175 Seasonal Recipes

Make the most of fresh ingredients through the year
with delicious dishes shown in 190 photographs

Editor: ANNE HILDYARD

southwater

This edition is published by Southwater, an imprint of Anness Publishing Ltd, Blaby Road, Wigston, Leicestershire LE18 4SE;

info@anness.com

Web: www.southwaterbooks.com; www.annesspublishing.com

If you like the images in this book and would like to investigate using them for publishing, promotions or advertising, please visit our website www.practicalpictures.com for more information.

Publisher: Joanna Lorenz
Editor: Anne Hildyard
Jacket Design: Nigel Partridge
Production Controller: Wendy Lawson

NOTES
Bracketed terms are intended for American readers.

For all recipes, quantities are given in both metric and imperial measures and, where appropriate, in standard cups and spoons. Follow one set of measures, but not a mixture, because they are not interchangeable.

Standard spoon and cup measures are level. 1 tsp = 5ml, 1 tbsp = 15ml, 1 cup = 250ml/8fl oz. Australian standard tablespoons are 20ml. Australian readers should use 3 tsp in place of 1 tbsp for measuring small quantities.

American pints are 16fl oz/2 cups. American readers should use 20fl oz/2.5 cups in place of 1 pint when measuring liquids. Electric oven temperatures in this book are for conventional ovens. When using a fan oven, the temperature will probably need to be reduced by about 10–20°C/20–40°F. Since ovens vary, you should check with your manufacturer's instruction book for guidance. The nutritional analysis given for each recipe is calculated per portion (i.e. serving or item), unless otherwise stated. If the recipe gives a range, such as Serves 4–6, then the nutritional analysis will be for the smaller portion size, i.e. 6 servings. The analysis does not include optional ingredients, such as salt added to taste. Medium (US large) eggs are used unless otherwise stated.

Previously published as part of a larger volume,
500 Seasonal Recipes

Contents

Introduction

Apart from the fact that seasonal food is fresher, tastes better and plays a hugely important role in a healthy diet because it is more nutritious, there are other good reasons to eat seasonally. It is quite exciting to look forward to the first peas or new potatoes of the season, and fruit and vegetables that are left to ripen naturally will have more flavour than those ripened artificially. If we buy locally grown food, there will be a much shorter time from picking to your shopping basket. Seasonal food can be found at supermarkets,

and farmer's markets are also a good source of producers who do not grow food intensively. There is little point in buying vegetables such as asparagus that has been flown halfway across the world, with the resultant loss of vitamins, when a product of much higher quality is available locally for several months of the year. Vegetable boxes are another way of getting a good variety of seasonal food, and they can be delivered to your door every week. You can buy organic produce, which should be more wholesome as it is naturally grown or reared, in the knowledge that the animals are raised or caught in a humane, ethically responsible manner. 'Pick your own' farms are fun for the whole family, and you can make sure all the fruits and vegetables are good quality, plus they could not be fresher!

There is nothing so delicious as fruits that are harvested when ripe and sweet, but sometimes exotic fruits such as pineapples, bananas and passion fruits are needed when seasonal fruits are scarce.

This appealing book provides a taste of a range of dishes from every season of the year. The wealth of different recipes shows that it is easy to choose seasonal foods, and when the season for one ingredient is over, another will tempt the tastebuds. Once you have eaten through a year of seasonal food, you will find it becomes second nature and the variety of foods means you will never be bored. After the cold dark days of winter, spring heralds the first spinach, asparagus, spring greens, spring onions, lamb and rhubarb, providing ingredients for lighter, greener dishes. To celebrate the return of spring, try Grilled Spring Onions and Asparagus with Parma Ham, the classic Roasted Leg of Lamb with Rosemary and Garlic, and Rhubarb and

Raspberry Crumble to follow. In summer, berries, garden peas and sweet tomatoes make an appearance: enjoy dishes such as Summer Pea and Chive Soup, Tomato Salad with Marinated Peppers and Oregano, Salted and Grilled Sardines, and to finish, Chocolate Redcurrant Torte. For the colder, shorter days of autumn, make warming dishes such as Sweet Potato and Parsnip Soup, Warm Halloumi and Fennel Salad, Spicy Root Vegetable Gratin, Mushroom Stroganoff, Hunter's Stew, then for a

grand finale, Butternut Squash and Maple Pie. Winter is the opportunity to cook some serious comfort food: hearty Kale, Chorizo and Potato Soup, Leek and Onion Tartlets, Winter Coleslaw, Chicken with Winter Vegetables, Turkey Croquettes, and Winter Cheesecake with a Pomegranate Glaze.

The 175 recipes in the book are divided into seasons so that you can plan your meals with the best available ingredients. Each chapter features every kind of dish, from soups and appetizers to vegetable, meat and fish dishes, and includes desserts and healthy drinks and juices.

Whatever the occasion, you can be sure of finding recipes that will ensure you eat well throughout the year.

Chilled Avocado Soup with Cumin

This chilled avocado soup, which is also known as green gazpacho, was invented in Spain. This mild, creamy soup is packed with the flavours of spring.

Serves 4
3 ripe avocados
1 bunch spring onions (scallions), white parts only, trimmed and roughly chopped
2 garlic cloves, chopped
juice of 1 lemon
1.5ml/¼ tsp ground cumin
1.5ml/¼ tsp paprika
450ml/¾ pint/scant 2 cups fresh chicken stock, cooled, and all fat skimmed off
300ml/½ pint/1¼ cups iced water
salt and ground black pepper
roughly chopped fresh flat leaf parsley, to serve

1 Starting half a day, or several hours, ahead to allow time for chilling, put the flesh of one avocado in a food processor or blender. Add the spring onions, garlic and lemon juice and purée until smooth.

2 Add the second avocado and purée, then the third, with the spices and seasoning. Purée until smooth.

3 Gradually add the chicken stock. Pour the soup into a metal bowl or other suitable container and chill.

4 To serve, stir in the iced water, then season to taste with plenty of salt and black pepper. Garnish with chopped parsley and serve immediately.

Cook's Tip
When avocados are plentiful and inexpensive, peel them, remove their stones (pits) and mash the flesh with lemon juice, then place in small containers in the freezer. Thaw in the refrigerator and use to make soups or dips.

Watercress Soup

Watercress and garden cress are nutritious aquatic leaf vegetables that can commonly be found growing wild in the spring. The peppery flavour of cress makes it ideal for sauces, salads and soups.

Serves 4
25g/1oz/2 tbsp unsalted butter or vegetable oil
1 large onion, chopped
1 leek, white part only, chopped
1 garlic clove, roughly chopped
2 large potatoes, peeled and cubed
1.5 litres/2½ pints/6¼ cups hot chicken or vegetable stock
1 bay leaf
1 large bunch of watercress, well rinsed, large stems removed, roughly chopped
1 large bunch of garden cress, rinsed, large stems removed, chopped (see Cook's Tip)
salt and ground black pepper
50g/2oz watercress leaves, to garnish

1 Heat the butter or oil in a large pan over medium-high heat. Stir in the onion, then sauté for 2–3 minutes. Add the leek, garlic and potatoes. Sauté for 5 minutes more, stirring until the mixture becomes fragrant.

2 Pour in the chicken or vegetable stock and add the bay leaf. Bring to the boil, reduce the heat to medium-low, cover and simmer for 20–30 minutes, until the potatoes are tender.

3 Stir in the watercress and garden cress. Simmer, uncovered, for 3 minutes and no longer, to preserve the fresh green colour and cook the cress lightly.

4 Remove the bay leaf. With a hand-held blender or in a food processor, purée the soup until smooth or until it reaches the desired consistency. Season to taste with salt and pepper.

5 Reheat if necessary, ladle into warm bowls and serve, garnished with fresh watercress leaves.

Cook's Tip
If you can't locate garden cress, use two bunches of watercress.

Chilled Avocado Soup Energy 148kcal/613kJ; Protein 1.9g; Carbohydrate 2.2g, of which sugars 1.1g; Fat 14.6g, of which saturates 3.1g; Cholesterol 0mg; Calcium 18mg; Fibre 2.9g; Sodium 6mg.
Watercress Soup Energy 598kcal/2515kJ; Protein 19.9g; Carbohydrate 76.3g, of which sugars 14.3g; Fat 25.9g, of which saturates 14.5g; Cholesterol 53mg; Calcium 602mg; Fibre 13.7g; Sodium 348mg.

Bacon and Leek Soup

Traditionally, this often made two courses or even two meals – the bacon and vegetables for one and the broth for the other.

Serves 4–6
1 piece unsmoked bacon, weighing about 1kg/2¼lb

500g/1lb 2oz/4½ cups leeks
1 large carrot, finely chopped
1 large potato, sliced
15ml/1 tbsp fine or medium oatmeal
handful of fresh parsley
salt and ground black pepper

1 Trim the bacon of excess fat, put it in a large pan and pour over enough cold water to cover. Bring to the boil, then discard the water. Add 1.5 litres/2¾ pints cold water, bring to the boil, then cover and simmer gently for 30 minutes.

2 Thickly slice the white and pale green parts of the leeks, reserving the dark green leaves. Add the sliced leek to the pan with the carrot, potato and oatmeal. Bring the soup back to the boil. Cover the pan and simmer gently for a further 30–40 minutes, until the vegetables and bacon are tender.

3 Slice the reserved dark green leeks very thinly and finely chop the parsley.

4 Lift the bacon out of the pan and either slice it and serve separately or cut it into bitesize chunks and stir these back into the soup.

5 Adjust the seasoning to taste, adding pepper, but it may not be necessary to add salt. Bring the soup to the boil. Add the sliced dark green leeks and parsley, and simmer very gently for about 5 minutes before serving.

> **Variation**
> *A chunk of beef or lamb may be used instead of the bacon, and other root vegetables may be added. Shredded cabbage is also popular.*

Asparagus and Pea Soup

This bright and tasty soup is ideal for using up bundles of fresh asparagus during the short spring harvest.

Serves 6
350g/12oz asparagus
2 leeks
1 bay leaf
1 carrot, roughly chopped
1 celery stick, chopped
few stalks of fresh parsley

1.75 litres/3 pints/7½ cups cold water
25g/1oz/2 tbsp butter
150g/5oz fresh garden peas
15ml/1 tbsp chopped fresh parsley
120ml/4fl oz/½ cup double (heavy) cream
grated rind of ½ lemon
salt and ground black pepper
shavings of Parmesan cheese, to serve

1 Cut the woody ends from the asparagus, then set the spears aside. Roughly chop the woody ends and place them in a large pan. Cut off and chop the green parts of the leeks and add to the asparagus stalks with the bay leaf, carrot, celery, parsley stalks and the cold water. Bring to the boil and simmer for about 30 minutes. Strain the stock and discard the vegetables.

2 Cut the tips off the asparagus and set aside, then cut the stems into short pieces. Chop the remainder of the leeks.

3 Melt the butter in a large pan and add the leeks. Cook for 3–4 minutes until softened. Add the asparagus stems, peas and parsley. Pour in 1.2 litres/2 pints/5 cups of the asparagus stock. Boil, reduce the heat and cook for 6–8 minutes. Season well.

4 Purée the soup in a food processor or blender. Press through a fine sieve (strainer) into the rinsed-out pan. Stir in the cream and lemon rind.

5 Bring a small pan of water to the boil and cook the asparagus tips for 2–3 minutes or until tender. Drain and refresh under cold water. Reheat the soup, but do not boil.

6 Ladle the soup into six warmed bowls and garnish with the asparagus tips. Serve with Parmesan cheese and black pepper.

Bacon and Leek Soup Energy 337kcal/1422kJ; Protein 51.4g; Carbohydrate 11.3g, of which sugars 3.3g; Fat 10g, of which saturates 3.6g; Cholesterol 33mg; Calcium 44mg; Fibre 2.7g; Sodium 1860mg.
Asparagus and Pea Soup Energy 184kcal/759kJ; Protein 4.9g; Carbohydrate 7.2g, of which sugars 4.4g; Fat 15.3g, of which saturates 9.1g; Cholesterol 36mg; Calcium 56mg; Fibre 3.9g; Sodium 39mg.

Apple and Leek Relish

Fresh and tangy, this simple relish of sliced leeks and apples with a lemon and honey dressing can be served with a range of cold meats as part of a spring buffet or for a springtime barbecue when the weather is good enough to eat outdoors. For the best result, make sure you use slim young leeks and tart, crisp apples.

Serves 4
2 slim leeks, white part only, washed thoroughly
2 large apples
15ml/1 tbsp chopped fresh parsley
juice of 1 lemon
15ml/1 tbsp clear honey
salt and ground black pepper, to taste

1 Thinly slice the leeks. Peel and core the apples, then slice the flesh thinly.

2 Place the sliced leek and apple into a large serving bowl and add the fresh parsley, lemon juice and honey. Season to taste with salt and ground black pepper.

3 Toss the ingredients thoroughly with two wooden spoons until they are well combined. Leave the bowl to stand in a cool place for about an hour before serving, to allow the flavours to blend together.

Variation
This relish could also be made with a mixture of pears and apples, if you prefer. The variation in texture between the softer pear slices and the crisp, tart apples will add extra interest to the relish.

Cook's Tip
When buying leeks, look for slim ones with firm white stems and bright green leaves. Avoid those that are discoloured in any way.

Guacamole

One of the best-loved Mexican salsas, this blend of creamy avocado, tomatoes, chillies, coriander and lime now appears on tables the world over. Ready-made guacamole usually contains mayonnaise, which helps to preserve the avocado, but this is not an ingredient in traditional recipes.

Serves 6–8
4 medium tomatoes
4 ripe avocados, preferably fuerte
juice of 1 lime
1/2 small onion
2 garlic cloves
small bunch of fresh coriander (cilantro), chopped
3 fresh red fresno chillies
salt
tortilla chips, to serve

1 Cut a cross in the base of each tomato. Place the tomatoes in a heatproof bowl and pour over boiling water to cover.

2 Leave the tomatoes in the water for 3 minutes, then lift them out using a slotted spoon and plunge them into a bowl of cold water. Drain. The skins will have begun to peel back from the crosses. Remove the skins completely. Cut the tomatoes in half, remove the seeds with a teaspoon, then chop the flesh roughly and set it aside.

3 Cut the avocados in half then remove the stones (pits). Scoop the flesh out of the shells and place it in a food processor or blender. Process until almost smooth, then scrape into a bowl and stir in the lime juice.

4 Chop the onion finely, then crush the garlic. Add both to the avocado and mix well. Stir in the coriander.

5 Remove the stalks from the chillies, slit them and scrape out the seeds with a small sharp knife. Chop the chillies finely and add them to the avocado mixture, with the chopped tomatoes. Mix well.

6 Check the seasoning and add salt to taste. Cover closely with clear film (plastic wrap) or a tight-fitting lid and chill for 1 hour before serving as a dip with tortilla chips. If it is well covered, guacamole will keep in the refrigerator for 2–3 days.

Salsa Verde

There are many versions of this classic green salsa. Try this springtime version drizzled over chargrilled squid, or with jacket potatoes served with a green spring salad.

Serves 4

2–4 fresh green chillies, halved
8 spring onions (scallions)

2 garlic cloves
50g/2oz salted capers
sprig of fresh tarragon
bunch of fresh parsley
grated rind and juice of 1 lime
juice of 1 lemon
90ml/6 tbsp olive oil
about 15ml/1 tbsp green
   Tabasco sauce
ground black pepper

1 Halve and seed the chillies and trim the spring onions. Halve the garlic cloves. Place in a food processor and pulse briefly.

2 Use your fingers to rub the excess salt off the capers. Add them, with the tarragon and parsley, to the food processor and pulse again until the ingredients are quite finely chopped.

3 Transfer the mixture to a bowl. Mix in the lime rind and juice, lemon juice and olive oil, stirring lightly so the citrus juice and oil do not emulsify.

4 Add the green Tabasco sauce, a little at a time, and ground black pepper to taste.

5 Chill the salsa in the refrigerator until ready to serve, but do not prepare it more than 8 hours in advance.

Cook's Tips
• Some salted capers are quite strong and may need rinsing in water before use. If you prefer, you can use pickled capers in the recipe instead.
• If you prefer a little more fire in your salsa verde then simply increase the amount of green Tabasco sauce to taste.
• Take care not to touch your eyes after chopping chillies because the oil from the chillies will cause irritation.

Grilled Spring Onions

Spring onions mark the return of better weather, and this simple dish is the perfect way to serve them.

Serves 6

3 bunches plump spring
   onions (scallions)
olive oil, for brushing

For the romesco sauce
2–3 mild dried red chillies
1 large red (bell) pepper, halved
   and seeded

2 tomatoes, halved and seeded
4–6 large garlic cloves, unpeeled
75–90ml/5–6 tbsp olive oil
25g/1oz/¼ cup hazelnuts,
   blanched
4 slices French bread, each about
   2cm/¾in thick
15ml/1 tbsp sherry vinegar
squeeze of lemon juice (optional)
chopped fresh parsley, to garnish

1 Prepare the sauce. Soak the dried chillies in hot water for about 30 minutes. Preheat the oven to 220°C/425°F/Gas 7.

2 Place the pepper, tomatoes and garlic on a baking sheet and drizzle with 15ml/1 tbsp oil. Roast, uncovered, for 35 minutes, until the pepper is blistered and blackened and the garlic is soft. Cool slightly, then peel the pepper, tomatoes and garlic.

3 Heat the remaining oil in a frying pan and fry the hazelnuts until lightly browned, then transfer to a plate. Fry the bread in the same oil until light brown on both sides, then transfer to the plate with the nuts and leave to cool. Reserve the oil.

4 Drain the chillies, discard the seeds, then place the chillies in a food processor. Add the peppers, tomatoes, garlic, hazelnuts and bread together with the reserved oil. Add the vinegar and process to a paste. Check the seasoning and set aside.

5 Trim the roots from the spring onions so that they are about 15–18cm/6–7in long. Brush with oil.

6 Heat an oiled ridged grill (broiler) pan and cook the onions for about 2 minutes on each side, turning once and brushing with oil. Serve immediately with the sauce.

Salsa Verde Energy 158kcal/652kJ; Protein 0.9g; Carbohydrate 1.1g, of which sugars 1g; Fat 16.8g, of which saturates 2.4g; Cholesterol 0mg; Calcium 35mg; Fibre 1g; Sodium 6mg.
Grilled Onions Energy 442kcal/1843kJ; Protein 8g; Carbohydrate 39.2g, of which sugars 3g; Fat 28.5g, of which saturates 3.3g; Cholesterol 0mg; Calcium 100mg; Fibre 2.5g; Sodium 121mg.

Spinach and Roast Garlic Salad

Don't worry about the amount of garlic in this spring salad. During roasting, the garlic becomes sweet and subtle and loses its strong, pungent taste.

450g/1lb baby spinach leaves
50g/2oz/1/2 cup pine nuts, lightly toasted
juice of 1/2 lemon
salt and ground black pepper

Serves 4
12 garlic cloves, unpeeled
60ml/4 tbsp extra virgin olive oil

1 Preheat the oven to 190°C/375°F/Gas 5. Place the garlic in a small roasting pan, toss in 30ml/2 tbsp of the olive oil and roast for about 15 minutes, until the garlic cloves are slightly charred around the edges.

2 While still warm, transfer the roasted garlic to a large salad bowl. Add the spinach leaves, pine nuts and lemon juice, along with the remaining olive oil and a little salt. Toss well and add ground black pepper to taste.

3 Serve the salad immediately, inviting guests to squeeze the softened garlic purée out of the skin to eat.

Variation
You can use a mixture of young spinach leaves and other spring salad leaves, if you prefer, for this salad. Try combining the spinach leaves with a handful of watercress or rocket (arugula) leaves.

Cook's Tip
The spinach leaves need to be young and tender for this salad. Packets of baby spinach are often sold in the salad sections of supermarkets, or look out for them appearing in local grocers in the springtime.

Globe Artichoke Salad

This salad first course is a great way to make the most of artichokes. It is equally good served hot or cold.

900ml/1 1/2 pints/3 3/4 cups home-made vegetable stock and water mixed
2 garlic cloves, chopped
1 small bunch parsley
6 whole peppercorns
15ml/1 tbsp olive oil, plus extra for drizzling

Serves 4
4 artichokes
juice of 1 lemon

1 To prepare the artichokes, trim the stalks of the artichokes close to the base, cut the very tips off the leaves and then divide them into quarters. Remove the inedible hairy choke (the central part), carefully scraping the hairs away from the heart at the base of the artichoke.

2 Squeeze a little of the lemon juice over the cut surfaces of the artichokes to prevent discoloration.

3 Put the artichokes into a pan and cover with the stock and water, garlic, parsley, peppercorns and olive oil. Cover with a lid and cook gently for 1 hour, or until the artichokes are tender. They are ready when the leaves come away easily when pulled.

4 Remove the artichokes with a slotted spoon. Boil the cooking liquid hard to reduce by half, then strain.

5 To serve, arrange the artichokes in small serving dishes and pour over the reduced juices. Drizzle over a little extra olive oil and lemon juice. Provide finger bowls and a bowl for the leaves.

6 To eat, pull a leaf away from the artichoke and scrape the fleshy part at the base with your teeth. Discard the remainder of the leaves and then eat the heart at the base.

Variation
If you can find tiny purple artichokes with tapered leaves, they can be cooked and eaten whole as the chokes are very tender.

Spinach and Garlic Salad Energy 234kcal/966kJ; Protein 6.1g; Carbohydrate 6g, of which sugars 3.7g; Fat 20.8g, of which saturates 2.3g; Cholesterol 0mg; Calcium 240mg; Fibre 4.6g; Sodium 23mg.
Globe Artichoke Salad Energy 59kcal/245kJ; Protein 0.7g; Carbohydrate 7.8g, of which sugars 7.3g; Fat 3.1g, of which saturates 0.5g; Cholesterol 0mg; Calcium 25mg; Fibre 2.4g; Sodium 61mg.

Grilled Spring Onions and Asparagus with Parma Ham

This is a good choice of first course for mid to late spring, when both spring onions and asparagus are at their best. The smokiness of the grilled vegetables goes well with the sweetness of the air-dried ham.

500g/1¼lb asparagus
45–60ml/3–4 tbsp olive oil
20ml/4 tsp balsamic vinegar
8–12 slices Parma or San
   Daniele ham
50g/2oz Pecorino cheese
sea salt and ground black pepper
extra virgin olive oil, to serve

Serves 4–6
2 bunches (about 24) plump
   spring onions (scallions)

1 Trim the root, outer skin and the top off the spring onions. Cut off and discard the woody ends of the asparagus. Use a vegetable peeler to peel the bottom 7.5cm/3in of the spears.

2 Preheat the grill (broiler). Toss the spring onions and asparagus in 30ml/2 tbsp of the oil. Place on two baking sheets and season.

3 Grill (broil) the asparagus for 5 minutes on each side, until just tender when tested with the tip of a sharp knife. Protect the tips with foil if they seem to char too much.

4 Grill the spring onions for about 3–4 minutes on each side, until tinged with brown. Brush the vegetables with more oil as you turn them.

5 Arrange the vegetables on individual plates. Season with pepper and drizzle over the vinegar. Lay 2–3 slices of ham on each plate and shave the Pecorino over the top.

Cook's Tip
If more convenient, the trimmed and peeled asparagus spears can be roasted at 200°C/400°F/Gas 6 for 15 minutes.

Broad Bean Salad

The Moroccan technique of marrying broad beans with preserved lemons creates a flavourful side salad.

Serves 4
2kg/4½lb broad (fava) beans
   in the pod
60–75ml/4–5 tbsp olive oil

juice of ½ lemon
2 garlic cloves, chopped
5ml/1 tsp ground cumin
10ml/2 tsp paprika
small bunch of fresh
   coriander (cilantro)
1 preserved lemon, chopped
handful of black olives, to garnish
salt and ground black pepper

1 Bring a large pan of salted water to the boil. Meanwhile, pod the broad beans. Put the shelled beans in the pan and boil for about 2 minutes.

2 Drain and refresh the beans under cold running water. Drain well. Slip off and discard the thick outer skin to reveal the smooth, bright green beans underneath.

3 Put the beans in a heavy pan and add the olive oil, lemon juice, garlic, cumin and paprika. Cook the beans gently over a low heat for about 10 minutes, then season to taste with salt and pepper and leave to cool in the pan until warm.

4 Transfer the beans to a serving bowl, and add the pan juices. Finely chop the coriander and add to the beans with the lemon. Toss, then garnish with the black olives and serve immediately.

Cook's Tip
To make preserved lemons, scrub and quarter lemons almost through to the base, then rub the cut sides with salt. Pack tightly into a large sterilized jar. Half fill the jar with more salt, adding some bay leaves, peppercorns and cinnamon, if you like. Cover completely with lemon juice. Cover with a lid and store for 2 weeks, shaking the jar daily. Add a little olive oil to seal and use within 1–6 months, washing off the salt before use.

Grilled Spring Onions Energy 109kcal/450kJ; Protein 8g; Carbohydrate 2.9g, of which sugars 2.8g; Fat 7.3g, of which saturates 1.4g; Cholesterol 15mg; Calcium 47mg; Fibre 1.9g; Sodium 312mg.
Broad Bean Salad Energy 272kcal/1143kJ; Protein 16.6g; Carbohydrate 24.6g, of which sugars 2.9g; Fat 12.7g, of which saturates 1.8g; Cholesterol 0mg; Calcium 142mg; Fibre 13.6g; Sodium 21mg.

Scrambled Eggs with Asparagus

Delightfully tender fresh asparagus and sweet peas are full of the taste of spring, and make perfect partners to eggs. The secret of scrambling is to keep the heat under the pan low and serve the eggs while they are still creamy.

Serves 4
1 bunch thin asparagus
30–45ml/2–3 tbsp tiny raw mangetouts (snow peas)
8 large (US extra large) eggs
30ml/2 tbsp milk
50g/2oz/¼ cup butter
salt and ground black pepper
sweet paprika, for dusting

1 Prepare the asparagus. Using a large sharp knife, cut off and discard any hard stems. Cut the stems into short lengths, keeping the tips separate. Shell some of the fatter mangetout pods, to extract the tiny peas.

2 Place the stems into a pan of boiling water and simmer for about 4 minutes. Add the asparagus tips, and cook for another 4–6 minutes. If including some pea pod strips, cook them for about 2 minutes.

3 Break the eggs into a bowl. Add the milk, salt and black pepper and beat with a whisk until well combined.

4 Melt the butter in a large frying pan and pour in the eggs, scrambling them by pulling the cooked outsides to the middle with a wooden spoon.

5 When the eggs are almost cooked, drain the asparagus and pea pod strips, if using, and stir them gently into the eggs. Sprinkle the peas over the top, and dust lightly with a little paprika. Serve immediately.

Variation
You can replace the asparagus with mangetouts (snow peas) if you are unable to find any. Remove any strings from 150g/5oz mangetouts, then slice them diagonally into two or three pieces. Cook in boiling water for 2 minutes.

Cheese and Asparagus Flan

The asparagus season in spring is short, so you need to make the most of it with this delicious flan.

Serves 5–6
175g/6oz/1½ cups plain (all-purpose) flour
40g/1½oz/3 tbsp lard or white cooking fat, diced

40g/1½oz/3 tbsp butter, diced
300g/11oz asparagus spears
75g/3oz mature (sharp) Cheddar cheese, grated
3 spring onions (scallions), sliced
2 eggs
300ml/½ pint/1¼ cups double (heavy) cream
freshly grated nutmeg
salt and ground black pepper

1 To make the pastry, sift the flour and a pinch of salt into a bowl and add the lard and butter. With your fingertips, rub the fats into the flour until the mixture resembles fine breadcrumbs. Stir in 45ml/3 tbsp cold water until the mixture can be gathered together into a ball. Wrap and chill for 30 minutes.

2 Put a flat baking sheet in the oven and preheat to 200°C/400°F/Gas 6. Roll out the pastry on a lightly floured work surface and use it to line a 20cm/8in flan tin (pan).

3 Line the pastry case (pie shell) with baking parchment and add a layer of baking beans. Put the tin on to the baking sheet in the oven and cook for 10–15 minutes until set. Remove the beans and parchment, return the pastry to the oven and cook for a further 5 minutes, until light golden brown. Remove the flan and reduce the temperature to 180°C/350°F/Gas 4.

4 Meanwhile, cook the asparagus in lightly salted boiling water for 2–3 minutes until only just tender. Drain, rinse and pat dry. Cut the spears into 2.5cm/1in lengths, leaving the tips whole.

5 Sprinkle half the cheese in the base of the cooked pastry case and add the asparagus and the spring onions. Beat the eggs with the cream and season with salt, pepper and nutmeg. Pour over the asparagus and top with the remaining cheese.

6 Return the flan to the oven and cook for 30 minutes or until just set. Leave for 5 minutes before cutting and serving.

Scrambled Eggs Energy 252kcal/1045kJ; Protein 13.8g; Carbohydrate 1.3g, of which sugars 1.2g; Fat 21.7g, of which saturates 9.7g; Cholesterol 408mg; Calcium 78mg; Fibre 0.6g; Sodium 219mg.
Cheese Flan Energy 547kcal/2266kJ; Protein 10.4g; Carbohydrate 24.7g, of which sugars 2.4g; Fat 45.6g, of which saturates 26.2g; Cholesterol 165mg; Calcium 184mg; Fibre 1.8g; Sodium 167mg.

Garganelli with Spring Vegetables

Fresh, brightly coloured
spring vegetables both look
and taste good when served
with pasta.

Serves 4
1 bunch asparagus, about
    350g/12oz
4 young carrots
1 bunch spring onions (scallions)
130g/4½oz shelled fresh peas

350g/12oz/3 cups dried
    garganelli
60ml/4 tbsp dry white wine
90ml/6 tbsp extra virgin olive oil
a few sprigs fresh flat leaf parsley,
    mint and basil, leaves stripped
    and chopped
sea salt and ground black pepper
freshly grated Parmesan cheese or
    premium Italian-style vegetarian
    cheese, to serve

1 Trim off and discard the woody part of each asparagus stem,
then cut off the tips on the diagonal. Cut the stems on the
diagonal into 4cm/1½in pieces. Cut the carrots and spring
onions on the diagonal into similar-sized pieces.

2 Bring a large pan of lightly salted water to the boil. Add the
carrots, peas, asparagus stems and tips. Bring the water back to
the boil, then reduce the heat and simmer the vegetables for
about 6–8 minutes, until tender. The asparagus tips will cook
quickly, so remove them from the pan with a slotted spoon as
soon as they are ready.

3 Meanwhile, cook the pasta in salted boiling water for
10–12 minutes, or according to the instructions on the packet,
until the garganelli are just tender.

4 Drain the asparagus, carrots and peas and return them to
the pan. Add the white wine, olive oil and sea salt and black
pepper to taste, then gently toss over medium to high heat
until the white wine has reduced and the vegetables glisten
with the olive oil.

5 Drain the garganelli and transfer it into a warmed large bowl.
Add the vegetables, spring onions and fresh herbs and toss well.

6 Divide the pasta among four warmed individual plates and
serve immediately, with freshly grated cheese.

Peas and Carrots with Bacon

Springtime lets you indulge
in one of the season's treats:
fresh peas. Sweet and
tender, they are delicious
eaten raw, or can be
accompanied by young
carrots, pearl onions, garden
lettuce and salty bacon or
cured ham. This dish is
especially good served with
roast pork or beef for a
traditional Sunday meal.

40g/1½oz/3 tbsp butter
115g/4oz rindless smoked bacon,
    cut into fine strips
100g/3¾oz/⅔ cup baby or
    small pearl onions, peeled and
    left whole
100ml/3½fl oz/scant ½ cup
    chicken stock
1 small lettuce, cut in thin strips
pinch of sugar and grated nutmeg
salt and ground black pepper
chopped fresh parsley, to
    garnish, optional

Serves 4–6
8 young carrots, thinly sliced
1.6kg/3½lb fresh peas in pods or
    575g/1¼lb/5 cups frozen peas

1 Bring a pan of salted water to the boil. Add the carrots and
cook for 3 minutes. Remove with a slotted spoon and set aside.

2 Pod the peas and add them to the pan of boiling water.
Cook for 2 minutes, then drain and add the peas to a bowl of
iced water to stop them from cooking any further. Drain and
set aside.

3 Melt 25g/1oz/2 tbsp of the butter in a large frying pan. Add
the bacon and sauté for 3 minutes, then add the onions and
sauté for 4 minutes. When the onions are translucent, add the
carrots and sauté for 3 minutes until they are glazed.

4 Pour in the stock, cover and cook for 10–15 minutes, or until
all the liquid has been absorbed. Add the lettuce and cook
for 3–5 minutes until the strips have wilted.

5 Add the peas, with the remaining butter. Simmer for
2–3 minutes until the peas are just tender. Add the sugar and
nutmeg, season and stir to mix. Spoon into a warmed bowl,
garnish with parsley, if using, and serve.

Garganelli Energy 738kcal/3092kJ; Protein 29.5g; Carbohydrate 74g, of which sugars 5.2g; Fat 38.1g, of which saturates 10.4g; Cholesterol 38mg; Calcium 492mg; Fibre 4.3g; Sodium 416mg.
Peas and Carrots Energy 141kcal/585kJ; Protein 9.8g; Carbohydrate 15.5g, of which sugars 7.4g; Fat 4.9g, of which saturates 1.5g; Cholesterol 10mg; Calcium 49mg; Fibre 5.8g; Sodium 311mg.

Stir-fried Spring Greens

Garlic enhances the slightly bitter flavour of spring greens, and they taste great with bacon and chillies.

Serves 6
450g/1lb spring greens (collard)

15ml/1 tbsp vegetable oil
150g/5oz smoked streaky (fatty) bacon, in one piece
2 garlic cloves, crushed
1.5ml/¼ tsp crushed dried chillies
salt

1 Cut off the stalks from the greens. Lay the leaves flat on top of each other and roll into a cigar shape and slice very thinly. Heat the oil in a frying pan. Cut the bacon into small cubes and sauté gently in the oil for 5 minutes, or until golden brown. Lift out with a slotted spoon and drain on kitchen paper.

2 Increase the heat, add the crushed garlic and dried chillies to the oil remaining in the pan, and stir-fry for 30 seconds. Add the spring greens and toss until just tender. Season to taste with salt, stir in the bacon cubes and serve immediately.

Florets Polonaise

Spring vegetables become something very special with this pretty egg topping.

Serves 6
500g/1¼lb mixed vegetables, such as cauliflower, broccoli, romanesco and calabrese

50g/2oz/¼ cup butter
finely grated rind of ½ lemon
1 large garlic clove, crushed
25g/1oz/½ cup fresh breadcrumbs, lightly baked or grilled (broiled) until crisp
2 eggs, hard-boiled
sea salt and ground black pepper

1 Trim the vegetables and break into florets. Place in a steamer over a pan of boiling water for 5–7 minutes, until just tender. Toss in butter or oil and transfer to a serving dish.

2 Meanwhile, combine the lemon rind, garlic, seasoning and breadcrumbs. Finely chop the eggs and mix with the remaining ingredients. Sprinkle the mixture over the vegetables and serve.

Spring Asparagus with Egg

With a unique, delicious flavour, asparagus heralds the arrival of spring and its short season is celebrated with a range of delicious dishes such as this simple appetizer.

Serves 4
16 white or green asparagus spears

115g/4oz/½ cup clarified butter
4 hard-boiled eggs, finely chopped
grated rind and juice of ½ lemon
salt and ground black or white pepper
a handful of fresh parsley, chopped, to garnish

1 Trim the asparagus spears or snap them so that the tender stalk separates from the tougher base. Soak the spears in a bowl of cold water, refreshing the water a couple of times; this makes the stalks more juicy and easier to peel.

2 Bring a pan of salted water to the boil. Peel the asparagus if necessary (see Cook's Tip), and add the spears to the pan. Blanch the spears for about 5 minutes (depending on the thickness of the stalks) or until they are just tender.

3 Drain the asparagus and pat dry with kitchen paper. Arrange on individual plates or on a serving platter and keep warm.

4 Heat the clarified butter in a frying pan for about 3 minutes, until pale brown. Add the chopped hard-boiled eggs, and season with salt and pepper.

5 Cook the mixture for 45 seconds, stirring constantly, then add the lemon juice. Pour the mixture over the warm asparagus, sprinkle with the lemon rind and freshly chopped parsley and serve immediately.

Cook's Tip
Green asparagus seldom needs peeling but white asparagus has a tougher, woodier stem, so removing the tougher skin near the base improves the texture and lets the stalks cook evenly.

Stir-fried Greens Energy 106kcal/438kJ; Protein 5g; Carbohydrate 3.8g, of which sugars 3.7g; Fat 7.9g, of which saturates 2.2g; Cholesterol 16mg; Calcium 38mg; Fibre 1.6g; Sodium 320mg.
Florets Polonaise Energy 71kcal/297kJ; Protein 5.2g; Carbohydrate 4.7g, of which sugars 1.4g; Fat 3.6g, of which saturates 0.7g; Cholesterol 32mg; Calcium 57mg; Fibre 2.3g; Sodium 50mg.
Spring Asparagus Energy 313kcal/1289kJ; Protein 9.3g; Carbohydrate 2.2g, of which sugars 2.1g; Fat 29.8g, of which saturates 16.6g; Cholesterol 252mg; Calcium 61mg; Fibre 1.7g; Sodium 245mg.

Asparagus with Lemon Sauce

A simple egg and lemon dressing brings out the best in asparagus. Serve the asparagus as an appetizer or side dish; alternatively, enjoy it for a light supper, with bread and butter to mop up the juices.

Serves 4
675g/1½lb asparagus, tough
    ends removed, and tied in
    a bundle
15ml/1 tbsp cornflour (cornstarch)
2 egg yolks
juice of 1½ lemons
salt

1 Cook the bundle of asparagus in a tall pan of lightly salted, boiling water for 7–10 minutes.

2 Drain the asparagus well and arrange the spears in a large serving dish. Reserve about 200ml/7fl oz/scant 1 cup of the cooking liquid.

3 Blend the cornflour with the cooled, reserved cooking liquid then place in a small pan. Bring to the boil, stirring constantly, and cook over a gentle heat until the sauce thickens slightly. Remove the pan from the heat and leave to cool slightly.

4 Beat the egg yolks thoroughly with the lemon juice and gradually stir into the cooled sauce. Cook over very low heat, stirring constantly, until the sauce is fairly thick. Be careful not to overheat the sauce or it may curdle. As soon as the sauce has thickened, remove the pan from the heat and continue stirring for 1 minute. Taste and season with salt. Set aside the sauce to cool slightly.

5 Stir the cooled lemon sauce, then pour a little over the cooked asparagus. Cover the vegetables and chill in the refrigerator for at least 2 hours before serving with the rest of the sauce to accompany.

> **Cook's Tip**
> *For a slightly less tangy sauce, add a little caster (superfine) sugar with the salt in step 4.*

Risotto with Asparagus

Fresh farm asparagus only has a short spring season, so make the most of it in this tasty risotto.

Serves 3–4
225g/8oz fresh asparagus
750ml/1¼ pints/3 cups vegetable
    or chicken stock
65g/2½oz/5 tbsp butter
1 small onion, finely chopped
275g/10oz/1½ cups risotto rice,
    such as Arborio or Carnaroli
75g/3oz/1 cup freshly grated
    Parmesan cheese
salt and ground black pepper

1 Bring a pan of water to the boil. Cut off any woody pieces on the ends of the asparagus stalks, peel the lower portions, then cook in the water for 5 minutes. Drain the asparagus, reserving the cooking water, refresh under cold water and drain again. Cut the asparagus diagonally into 4cm/1½in pieces. Keep the tip and next-highest sections separate from the stalks.

2 Place the stock in a pan and add 450ml/¾ pint/scant 2 cups of the asparagus cooking water. Heat to simmering point, and keep it hot.

3 Melt two-thirds of the butter in a large, heavy pan or deep frying pan. Add the onion and fry until it is soft and golden.

4 Stir in all the asparagus except the top two sections. Cook for 2–3 minutes. Add the rice and cook for 1–2 minutes, mixing well to coat it with butter. Stir in a ladleful of the hot liquid. Using a wooden spoon, stir until the stock has been absorbed.

5 Gradually add the remaining stock, a little at a time, allowing the rice to absorb the liquid before adding more, and stirring all the time.

6 After 10 minutes, add the remaining asparagus sections. Continue to cook as before, for about 15 minutes, until the rice is al dente and the risotto is creamy.

7 Off the heat, stir in the remaining butter and the Parmesan. Grind in a little pepper, and taste for salt. Serve immediately.

Asparagus with Lemon Energy 96kcal/399kJ; Protein 6.4g; Carbohydrate 9.4g, of which sugars 5.8g; Fat 3.8g, of which saturates 1g; Cholesterol 101mg; Calcium 59mg; Fibre 2.9g; Sodium 8mg.
Asparagus Risotto Energy 629kcal/2616kJ; Protein 20.1g; Carbohydrate 71.9g, of which sugars 2.7g; Fat 27.9g, of which saturates 16.5g; Cholesterol 71mg; Calcium 344mg; Fibre 1.6g; Sodium 408mg.

Farfalle with Salmon and Dill

This quick, luxurious sauce for pasta has become very fashionable, but wherever you have it, it will taste delicious. Dill is the classic herb for cooking with fish, but if you don't like its aniseed flavour, substitute parsley or a little fresh tarragon. The fresher the herbs, the better the taste, so it is always worth growing some in pots or in the garden.

Serves 4
6 spring onions (scallions), sliced
50g/2oz/¼ cup butter
90ml/6 tbsp dry white wine
    or vermouth
450ml/¾ pint/scant 2 cups
    double (heavy) cream
freshly grated nutmeg
225g/8oz smoked salmon
30ml/2 tbsp chopped fresh dill
freshly squeezed lemon juice
450g/1lb/4 cups fresh farfalle
salt and ground black pepper
fresh dill sprigs, to garnish

1 Using a sharp cook's knife, slice the spring onions finely. Melt the butter in a large pan and fry the spring onions for about 1 minute, stirring occasionally, until softened.

2 Add the wine or vermouth to the pan. Increase the heat and bring the mixture to the boil. Let it boil vigorously to reduce the liquid to about 30ml/2 tbsp.

3 Stir in the cream and add salt, pepper and nutmeg to taste. Bring to the boil, then simmer for 2–3 minutes until thickened.

4 Cut the smoked salmon into 2.5cm/1in squares and stir into the sauce, together with the dill. Add lemon juice to taste.

5 Cook the pasta in a large pan of boiling salted water for 2–3 minutes, or until it rises to the surface of the liquid. Drain well. Toss with the sauce. Spoon into serving bowls and serve immediately, garnished with sprigs of dill.

> **Cook's Tip**
> If you can't find fresh pasta, use dried, and cook in boiling water for 12 minutes or according to the instructions on the packet.

Salmon with Asparagus

This spring dish is light and colourful. Asparagus makes the ideal accompaniment for salmon when it is in season. The hollandaise sauce requires concentration, but it's so good with both fresh salmon and asparagus, that it's well worth mastering.

Serves 4
bunch of 20 asparagus
    spears, trimmed

4 salmon portions, such as fillets
    or steaks, about 200g/7oz each
15ml/1 tbsp olive oil
juice of ½ lemon
25g/1oz/2 tbsp butter
salt and ground black pepper

For the hollandaise sauce
45ml/3 tbsp white wine vinegar
6 peppercorns
1 bay leaf
3 egg yolks
175g/6oz/¾ cup butter, softened

1 Peel the lower stems of the asparagus. Stand in a deep pan; cook in salted boiling water for about 1 minute, or until just beginning to become tender, then remove from the pan and cool quickly under cold running water to prevent further cooking. Drain.

2 To make the hollandaise sauce: in a small pan, boil the vinegar and 15ml/1 tbsp water with the peppercorns and bay leaf until reduced to 15ml/1 tbsp. Leave to cool. Cream the egg yolks with 15g/½oz/1 tbsp butter and a pinch of salt. Strain the vinegar into the eggs and set the bowl over a pan of boiling water. Remove from the heat.

3 Whisk in the remaining butter, no more than 10g/¼oz/1½ tsp at a time, until the sauce is shiny and has the consistency of thick cream. Season with salt and pepper.

4 Heat a ridged griddle pan or grill (broiler) until very hot. Brush the salmon with oil, sprinkle with the lemon juice and season. Cook the fish for 3–5 minutes on each side, depending on the thickness. The fish should be moist and succulent within.

5 Melt the butter in a separate large pan and gently reheat the asparagus in it for 1–2 minutes before serving with the fish and hollandaise sauce.

Farfalle with Salmon Energy 1162kcal/4846kJ; Protein 30g; Carbohydrate 86.5g, of which sugars 6.8g; Fat 77.4g, of which saturates 46.1g; Cholesterol 206mg; Calcium 104mg; Fibre 3.5g; Sodium 1180mg.
Salmon with Asparagus Energy 834kcal/3449kJ; Protein 46.5g; Carbohydrate 2.8g, of which sugars 2.7g; Fat 7.7g, of which saturates 31.6g; Cholesterol 358mg; Calcium 102mg; Fibre 2.1g; Sodium 401mg.

Teriyaki Salmon Fillets with Ginger Strips

Bottles of teriyaki sauce – a lovely rich Japanese glaze – are available in most large supermarkets and Asian stores. Serve the salmon with sticky rice or soba noodles for a healthy, light meal.

Serves 4

4 salmon fillets, 150g/5oz each
75ml/5 tbsp teriyaki marinade
150ml/¼ pint/⅔ cup
    sunflower oil
5cm/2in piece of fresh root
    ginger, peeled and cut into
    matchsticks

1 Put the salmon in a shallow, non-metallic dish and pour over the teriyaki marinade. Cover with clear film (plastic wrap) and chill for 2 hours.

2 Meanwhile, heat the sunflower oil in a small pan and add the ginger. Fry for 1–2 minutes, stirring constantly, until golden brown and crisp. Remove with a slotted spoon and drain on kitchen paper. Set aside until ready to serve the salmon.

3 Heat a griddle pan until smoking hot. Remove the salmon from the marinade and add, skin side down, to the pan. Cook for 2–3 minutes, then turn over and cook for a further 1–2 minutes, or until cooked through.

4 Remove from the pan and divide among four serving plates. Top the salmon fillets with the crispy fried ginger.

5 Pour the marinade into the pan and cook for 1–2 minutes. Pour over the salmon and serve immediately.

> ### Cook's Tip
> *In Japanese cuisine, teriyaki sauce is traditionally made by mixing and heating soy sauce, sake or mirin, and a sweetener such as sugar or honey. The sauce is reduced, then used to marinate meat which is then grilled or broiled. Sometimes ginger or garlic is added to the sauce.*

Salmon with Spicy Pesto

This is a great way to bone salmon steaks to give a solid piece of fish.

Serves 4

4 salmon steaks, each about
    225g/8oz
30ml/2 tbsp sunflower oil
finely grated rind and juice
    of 1 lime
salt and ground black pepper

lime wedges, to serve
red chilli, shredded finely

For the pesto
6 fresh mild red chillies, seeded
    and roughly chopped
2 garlic cloves
30ml/2 tbsp pumpkin or
    sunflower seeds
finely grated rind and juice of 1 lime
75ml/5 tbsp olive oil

1 Place a salmon steak flat on a board. Insert a very sharp knife close to the top of the bone. Staying close to the bone all the time, cut to the end of the steak to release one side of the steak. Repeat with the other side.

2 Place one piece of salmon skin side down and hold it firmly with one hand. Insert a small sharp knife between the skin the flesh and, working away from you, cut the flesh off in a single piece. Repeat with the remaining salmon steaks.

3 Wrap each piece of fish into a circle, with the thinner end wrapped around the fatter end. Tie with kitchen string. Place in a shallow bowl.

4 Rub the oil into the boneless fish rounds. Add the lime juice and rind to the bowl. Cover and marinate in the refrigerator for 2 hours.

5 Make the pesto. Put the chillies, garlic, pumpkin or sunflower seeds, lime rind and juice and seasoning into a food processor. Process until well mixed. With the machine running, gradually add the olive oil through the feeder tube. The pesto will slowly thicken and emulsify. Scrape it into a bowl. Preheat the grill (broiler).

6 Drain the salmon and place the rounds in a grill pan. Grill (broil) for 5 minutes on each side or until opaque. Serve with the spicy pesto and lime wedges. Garnish with chilli shreds.

Teriyaki Salmon Energy 239kcal/995kJ; Protein 24.8g; Carbohydrate 2.1g, of which sugars 1.7g; Fat 13.3g, of which saturates 2.3g; Cholesterol 58mg; Calcium 93mg; Fibre 0.3g; Sodium 323mg.
Salmon with Pesto Energy 653kcal/2719kJ; Protein 50.5g; Carbohydrate 1.4g, of which sugars 0.1g; Fat 49.6g, of which saturates 7.5g; Cholesterol 122mg; Calcium 60mg; Fibre 0.5g; Sodium 111mg.

White Fish Dumplings

Served on a bed of spring vegetables, these fish dumplings are delicious.

Serves 4
500g/1¼lb white fish fillets, diced, plus their bones
2 eggs, separated
5ml/1 tsp salt
2.5ml/½ tsp ground white pepper
a pinch of cayenne pepper
200ml/7fl oz/scant 1 cup double (heavy) cream
25ml/1½ tbsp vegetable oil
1 onion, chopped
1 small celery stick, chopped
300ml/½ pint/1¼ cups white wine
50g/2oz/¼ cup butter
30ml/2 tbsp plain (all-purpose) flour
15ml/1 tbsp chopped fresh dill
salt and ground black pepper
cooked spring vegetables, to serve

1 Place the diced fish in the bowl of a food processor and blend until finely chopped, slowly adding the egg whites, salt, pepper and cayenne pepper. Transfer to a bowl and place in the freezer for 20 minutes. Beat in 100ml/3½fl oz/scant ½ cup of the cream, then set aside in the refrigerator.

2 Heat the oil in a pan, add the onion and celery and fry for about 5 minutes, until softened. Add the fish bones and cook for 10 minutes. Pour in half of the wine and enough water to just cover the bones. Bring to the boil, then simmer for about 20 minutes. Strain the stock into a clean pan. You should have about 400ml/14fl oz/1⅔ cups. Bring back to the boil.

3 Shape the fish mixture into balls and add to the hot stock in batches. Cook for 5 minutes, turning them during cooking. When ready, remove with a slotted spoon and keep warm.

4 Melt the butter in a pan, stir in the flour to make a roux, then stir in a ladleful of the stock. Bring to the boil, stirring, until the sauce boils and thickens.

5 Stir the remaining wine and the remaining cream into the sauce, return to the boil, then remove from the heat. Whisk in the egg yolks and dill, then taste and add salt and pepper according to taste. Pour the sauce over the dumplings and serve hot, on a bed of cooked early summer vegetables.

Salmon Fishcakes

The secret of a good fishcake is to make it with freshly prepared fish and potatoes, home-made breadcrumbs and plenty of fresh herbs, such as dill and parsley or tarragon.

Serves 4
450g/1lb cooked salmon fillet
450g/1lb freshly cooked potatoes, mashed
25g/1oz/2 tbsp butter, melted or 30ml/2 tbsp olive oil
10ml/2 tsp wholegrain mustard
15ml/1 tbsp each chopped fresh dill and chopped fresh parsley or tarragon
grated rind and juice of ½ lemon
15g/½oz/2 tbsp wholemeal (whole-wheat) flour
1 egg, lightly beaten
150g/5oz/2 cups dried breadcrumbs
60ml/4 tbsp sunflower oil
sea salt and ground black pepper
rocket (arugula) leaves and chives, to garnish
lemon wedges, to serve

1 Flake the cooked salmon, discarding any skin and bones. Put it in a bowl with the mashed potato, melted butter or oil and wholegrain mustard, and mix well.

2 Stir the herbs and the lemon rind and juice into the fish and potato mixture. Season to taste with plenty of sea salt and ground black pepper.

3 Divide the mixture into eight portions and shape each into a ball, then flatten into a thick disc. Dip the fishcakes first in flour, then in egg and finally in breadcrumbs, making sure that they are evenly coated with crumbs.

4 Heat the oil in a frying pan until it is very hot. Fry the fishcakes in batches until golden brown and crisp all over. As each batch is ready, drain on kitchen paper and keep hot. Garnish with rocket and chives and serve with lemon wedges.

Cook's Tip
Any fresh white or hot-smoked fish is suitable. Always buy organically farmed fish, or sustainably caught wild fish.

Fish Dumplings Energy 600kcal/2484kJ; Protein 27.7g; Carbohydrate 6.5g, of which sugars 2.4g; Fat 46.4g, of which saturates 24.8g; Cholesterol 248mg; Calcium 73mg; Fibre 0.5g; Sodium 205mg.
Fishcakes Energy 586kcal/2453kJ; Protein 29.8g; Carbohydrate 49.9g, of which sugars 3.2g; Fat 31g, of which saturates 7.2g; Cholesterol 117mg; Calcium 79mg; Fibre 1.3g; Sodium 266mg.

Salted Salmon with Potatoes in Dill Sauce

Salted salmon is a refreshing alternative to the more commonly known gravlax recipe. This dish is delicious with potatoes and dill.

Serves 6–8
200g/7oz/2 cups sea salt
50g/2oz/½ cup caster
  (superfine) sugar
1kg/2¼lb salmon, scaled, filleted
  and boned
1 litre/1¾ pints/4 cups water
675–900g/1½–2lb new potatoes

For the béchamel and dill sauce
25g/1oz/2 tbsp butter
45ml/3 tbsp plain
  (all-purpose) flour
750ml/1¼ pints/3 cups milk
120ml/4fl oz/½ cup double
  (heavy) cream
freshly grated nutmeg (optional)
25g/1oz/¼ cup chopped fresh dill
salt and ground black pepper

1 Mix together 100g/4oz/1 cup of the salt and the sugar. Cover the fish fillets with the mixture and put in a plastic bag. Seal the bag and put the fish on a plate in the refrigerator overnight.

2 The next day, make a brine by mixing the remaining salt and the water in a bowl. Place the salmon in the brine and leave in the refrigerator for another night.

3 Remove the salmon from the brine and cut into 5mm/¼in slices. If large, cut the potatoes in half then cook in boiling water for about 20 minutes until tender.

4 Meanwhile, make the béchamel sauce. Melt the butter in a pan, add the flour and cook over low heat for 1 minute, stirring to make a roux. Remove from the heat and slowly add the milk, stirring all the time, to form a smooth sauce. Return to the heat and cook, stirring, for 2–3 minutes until the sauce boils and thickens. Stir in the cream, nutmeg if using, salt and pepper to taste and heat gently.

5 Drain the potatoes and add to the sauce with the dill. Serve the salted salmon with the potatoes in béchamel and dill.

Salmon Rolls with Asparagus and Butter Sauce

The green spears of asparagus appear each year as a welcome sign of spring. The green contrasts beautifully with the pink salmon in this recipe.

Serves 4
4 thick or 8 thin asparagus spears
4 very thin slices salmon fillet,
  each weighing about 115g/4oz
juice 1 lemon

1 bunch fresh parsley, chopped
salt and ground black pepper

For the butter sauce
1 shallot, finely chopped
6 peppercorns
120ml/4fl oz/½ cup dry white wine
60ml/4 tbsp double (heavy) cream
200g/7oz/scant 1 cup butter, cut
  into small cubes

1 Steam the asparagus spears for 6–8 minutes, according to their size, until tender. Refresh under cold running water, drain and set aside.

2 The slices of salmon should be wide enough to roll around the asparagus. Don't worry if they have to be patched together. Place the slices on a surface, season with salt and pepper, lay one or two asparagus spears across each slice and then roll the salmon around them. Place the rolls on a rack over a pan of boiling water, sprinkle with lemon juice, and cover and steam for 3–4 minutes until tender.

3 To make the butter sauce, put the shallot, peppercorns and wine in a small pan and heat gently until the wine has reduced to a tablespoonful. Strain and return to the pan. Add the cream, bring to the boil, and then lower the heat.

4 Add the butter to the sauce in small pieces, whisking all the time until well incorporated before adding another piece. Do not allow the sauce to boil or it will separate. Season the sauce to taste, if necessary.

5 Stir the chopped parsley into the sauce, and serve immediately with the salmon rolls.

Salted Salmon Energy 407kcal/1699kJ; Protein 26.4g; Carbohydrate 22.6g, of which sugars 5.9g; Fat 24g, of which saturates 9.7g; Cholesterol 85mg; Calcium 155mg; Fibre 1g; Sodium 118mg.
Salmon Rolls Energy 694kcal/2867kJ; Protein 25.7g; Carbohydrate 2.4g, of which sugars 2.1g; Fat 62.5g, of which saturates 33.4g; Cholesterol 187mg; Calcium 55mg; Fibre 0.6g; Sodium 362mg.

Roasted Duckling on a Bed of Honeyed Potatoes

The rich flavour of duck combined with these sweetened potatoes glazed with honey makes an excellent treat for a dinner party or special occasion.

Serves 4

1 duckling, giblets removed

60ml/4 tbsp light soy sauce
150ml/¼ pint/⅔ cup fresh orange juice
3 large floury potatoes, cut into chunks
30ml/2 tbsp clear honey
15ml/1 tbsp sesame seeds
salt and ground black pepper

1 Preheat the oven to 200°C/400°F/Gas 6. Place the duckling in a roasting pan. Prick the skin well all over with a fork.

2 Mix the soy sauce and orange juice together and pour over the duck. Cook in the oven for 20 minutes.

3 Place the potato chunks in a bowl and stir in the honey; toss to mix well. Remove the duckling from the oven and spoon the potatoes all around and under the duckling.

4 Roast for a further 35 minutes and remove from the oven. Toss the potatoes in the juices so the underside will be cooked and turn the duck over. Place back in the oven and cook for a further 30 minutes.

5 Remove the duckling from the oven and carefully scoop off the excess fat, leaving the juices behind.

6 Sprinkle the sesame seeds over the potatoes, season with salt and pepper and turn the duckling back over, breast side up, and cook for a further 10 minutes. Remove the duckling and potatoes from the oven and keep warm, allowing the duck to stand for a few minutes.

7 Pour off the excess fat and simmer the juices on the stove for a few minutes. Serve the juices with the carved duckling and the potatoes.

Duck and Sesame Stir-fry

For a special family meal that is a guaranteed success, this is ideal. It tastes fantastic and cooks fast, so you'll be eating in no time.

Serves 4

250g/9oz boneless duck meat
15ml/1 tbsp sesame oil
15ml/1 tbsp vegetable oil

4 garlic cloves, finely sliced
2.5ml/½ tsp dried chilli flakes
15ml/1 tbsp Thai fish sauce
15ml/1 tbsp light soy sauce
120ml/4fl oz/½ cup water
1 head broccoli, cut into small florets
coriander (cilantro) and 15ml/ 1 tbsp toasted sesame seeds, to garnish

1 Cut all the duck meat into bitesize pieces. Heat the oils in a wok or large, heavy frying pan and stir-fry the garlic over medium heat until it is golden brown – do not let it burn, otherwise it will give the food a bitter taste.

2 Add the duck to the pan and stir-fry for a further 2 minutes, until the meat begins to brown.

3 Stir in the chilli flakes, fish sauce, soy sauce and water. Add the broccoli and continue to stir-fry for about 2 minutes, until the duck is just cooked through.

4 Serve on warmed plates, garnished with coriander and the toasted sesame seeds.

Cook's Tip
Broccoli has excited interest recently since it is claimed that eating this dark green vegetable regularly can help to reduce the risk of some cancers. Broccoli is a source of protein, calcium, iron and magnesium, as well as vitamins A and C.

Variation
Pak choi (bok choy) or Chinese flowering cabbage can be used instead of broccoli.

Roasted Duckling Energy 806kcal/3341kJ; Protein 20.8g; Carbohydrate 32.3g, of which sugars 6.4g; Fat 66.8g, of which saturates 17.9g; Cholesterol 0mg; Calcium 53mg; Fibre 2.1g; Sodium 403mg.
Duck and Sesame Stir-fry Energy 165kcal/686kJ; Protein 17.4g; Carbohydrate 2.3g, of which sugars 2g; Fat 10.6g, of which saturates 1.8g; Cholesterol 69mg; Calcium 72mg; Fibre 2.9g; Sodium 345mg.

Chicken with Peas

This Italian dish strongly reflects the traditions of Mediterranean cuisine, and makes the most of tasty, seasonal spring produce.

Serves 4
4 skinless chicken breast fillets
plain (all-purpose) flour, for dusting
30–45ml/2–3 tbsp olive oil
1–2 onions, chopped
1/4 fennel bulb, chopped (optional)

15ml/1 tbsp chopped fresh parsley, plus extra to garnish
7.5ml/1 1/2 tsp fennel seeds
75ml/5 tbsp dry Marsala
120ml/4fl oz/1/2 cup chicken stock
300g/11oz/2 1/4 cups petits pois (baby peas)
juice of 1 1/2 lemons
2 egg yolks
salt and ground black pepper

1 Season the chicken with salt and pepper, then dust generously with flour. Shake off the excess flour; set aside.

2 Heat 15ml/1 tbsp oil in a pan, add the onions, fennel, if using, parsley and fennel seeds. Cook for 5 minutes.

3 Add the remaining oil and the chicken to the pan and cook for 2–3 minutes on each side, until lightly browned. Remove the chicken and onion mixture from the pan and set aside.

4 Deglaze the pan by pouring in the Marsala and cooking over a high heat until reduced to about 30ml/2 tbsp, then pour in the stock. Add the peas and return the chicken and onion mixture to the pan. Cook over very low heat while you prepare the egg mixture.

5 In a bowl, beat the lemon juice and egg yolks together, then gradually add about 120ml/4fl oz/1/2 cup of the hot liquid from the chicken and peas, stirring well to combine.

6 Return the mixture to the pan and cook over a low heat, stirring, until the mixture thickens slightly. (Do not allow the mixture to boil or the eggs will curdle and spoil the sauce.) Serve the chicken immediately, sprinkled with a little extra chopped fresh parsley.

Escalopes of Chicken with Vegetables

This is a quick and light dish – ideal for a sunny day in spring, when it is too hot to slave over the stove for hours or to eat heavy meals. Flattening the chicken breast fillets thins and tenderizes the meat and also speeds up the cooking process. The fresh tomato mayonnaise brings out the sweet flavour of the potatoes.

Serves 4
4 skinless chicken breast fillets, each weighing 175g/6oz

juice of 1 lime
120ml/4fl oz/1/2 cup olive oil
675g/1 1/2lb mixed baby potatoes, carrots, fennel (sliced if large), asparagus and peas
sea salt and ground black pepper
fresh flat leaf parsley sprigs, to garnish

For the tomato mayonnaise
150ml/1/4 pint/2/3 cup mayonnaise
15ml/1 tbsp sun-dried tomato paste

1 Lay the chicken portions between two sheets of clear film (plastic wrap) or baking parchment and beat them flat with a rolling pin. Season the chicken with salt and pepper and sprinkle with the lime juice.

2 Heat 45ml/3 tbsp of the oil in a frying pan or griddle pan and fry the chicken for 10 minutes on each side, or until cooked.

3 Meanwhile, put the potatoes and carrots in a pan with the remaining oil and season with sea salt. Cover and cook over medium heat for 10–15 minutes, stirring frequently.

4 Add the fennel to the pan of vegetables and cook for a further 5 minutes, stirring frequently. Finally, add the asparagus and peas and cook for 5 minutes more, or until all the vegetables are tender.

5 To make the sauce, mix together the mayonnaise and sun-dried tomato paste in a small bowl. Spoon the vegetables on to a warmed large serving platter or individual plates and arrange the chicken on top. Serve the tomato mayonnaise with the chicken and vegetables. Garnish with sprigs of flat leaf parsley.

Chicken with Peas Energy 319kcal/1338kJ; Protein 42g; Carbohydrate 9.1g, of which sugars 5.9g; Fat 10.7g, of which saturates 2.2g; Cholesterol 206mg; Calcium 67mg; Fibre 4.2g; Sodium 150mg.
Escalopes of Chicken Energy 513kcal/2143kJ; Protein 44g; Carbohydrate 18.9g, of which sugars 9g; Fat 29.6g, of which saturates 4.7g; Cholesterol 141mg; Calcium 41mg; Fibre 3.2g; Sodium 251mg.

Sweet-and-sour Lamb

Enjoy this simple dish when lamb appears in the stores.

Serves 4

8 French-trimmed lamb loin chops

90ml/6 tbsp balsamic vinegar
30ml/2 tbsp caster
    (superfine) sugar
30ml/2 tbsp olive oil
salt and ground black pepper

1 Put the lamb chops in a shallow, non-metallic dish and drizzle over the balsamic vinegar. Sprinkle with the sugar and season. Turn the chops to coat in the mixture, then cover with clear film (plastic wrap) and chill for 20 minutes.

2 Heat the olive oil in a large frying pan and add the chops, reserving the marinade. Cook for 3–4 minutes on each side. Pour the marinade into the pan and leave to bubble for about 2 minutes, or until reduced slightly. Remove from the pan and serve immediately.

Lamb with Oregano and Basil

Lamb leg steaks are chunky with a sweet flavour and go well with oregano and basil. However, you could also use finely chopped rosemary or thyme. Serve with couscous.

Serves 4

4 large or 8 small lamb leg steaks
60ml/4 tbsp garlic-infused olive oil
1 small bunch of fresh oregano, roughly chopped
1 small bunch of fresh basil, torn
salt and ground black pepper

1 Put the lamb in a shallow, non-metallic dish. Mix 45ml/3 tbsp of the oil with the oregano, basil and some salt and pepper, reserving some of the herbs for garnish. Pour over the lamb and turn to coat in the marinade. Cover and chill for up to 8 hours.

2 Heat the remaining oil in a large frying pan. Remove the lamb from the marinade and fry for 5–6 minutes on each side, until slightly pink in the centre. Add the marinade and cook for 1–2 minutes until warmed through. Garnish with the reserved herbs and serve.

Lamb Casserole with Broad Beans

This dish is ideal for using the abundance of lamb in spring. It is slowly simmered on top of the stove until the chunks of stewing lamb are meltingly tender. The casserole is flavoured with a large amount of garlic, and plenty of dry sherry adds richness to the sauce. The addition of broad beans adds attractive colour.

Serves 6

45ml/3 tbsp olive oil

1.3kg–1.6kg/3–3½lb lamb fillet,
    cut into 5cm/2in cubes
1 large onion, chopped
6 large garlic cloves, unpeeled
1 bay leaf
5ml/1 tsp paprika
120ml/4fl oz/½ cup dry sherry
115g/4oz shelled fresh or frozen
    broad (fava) beans
30ml/2 tbsp chopped fresh parsley
salt and ground black pepper
mashed or boiled potatoes,
    to serve (optional)

1 Heat 30ml/2 tbsp of the oil in a large flameproof casserole. Add half the lamb cubes to the pan and cook for 45 minutes until evenly browned on all sides. Transfer to a plate and set aside. Brown the rest of the meat in the same way and remove from the casserole.

2 Heat the remaining oil in the pan, add the onion and cook for about 5 minutes until softened and just beginning to turn brown. Return the browned lamb cubes to the casserole and stir in with the onion.

3 Add the garlic cloves, bay leaf, paprika and sherry to the casserole. Season with salt and ground black pepper. Bring the mixture to the boil, then reduce the heat. Cover the pan with a tight-fitting lid and simmer very gently for 1½–2 hours, until the meat is tender.

4 About 10 minutes before the end of the cooking time, stir in the broad beans. Re-cover the pan and place back in the oven until the meat and beans are tender.

5 Stir in the chopped parsley just before serving. Accompany the casserole with mashed or boiled potatoes, if you like.

Sweet-and-sour Lamb Energy 258kcal/1077kJ; Protein 19.6g; Carbohydrate 7.9g, of which sugars 7.9g; Fat 16.7g, of which saturates 6g; Cholesterol 76mg; Calcium 12mg; Fibre 0g; Sodium 87mg.
Lamb with Oregano Energy 466kcal/1938kJ; Protein 40g; Carbohydrate 0.7g, of which sugars 0.6g; Fat 33.7g, of which saturates 12g; Cholesterol 152mg; Calcium 66mg; Fibre 1.3g; Sodium 180mg
Lamb Casserole Energy 541kcal/2258kJ; Protein 50.8g; Carbohydrate 3.5g, of which sugars 1.2g; Fat 33.7g, of which saturates 13.8g; Cholesterol 190mg; Calcium 45mg; Fibre 1.6g; Sodium 221mg.

Herb-crusted Rack of Lamb with Puy Lentils

This lamb roast is quick and easy to prepare but looks impressive when served. It is the perfect choice for springtime entertaining. The delicate flavour of the lentils is the perfect complement to the rich meat.

Serves 4

2 x 6-bone racks of lamb, chined
50g/2oz/1 cup fresh white or
    wholemeal (whole-wheat)
    breadcrumbs
2 large garlic cloves, crushed

90ml/6 tbsp chopped mixed fresh
    herbs, plus sprigs to garnish
50g/2oz/¼ cup butter, melted or
    50ml/3½ tbsp olive oil
sea salt and ground black pepper
new potatoes, to serve

For the puy lentils

1 red onion, chopped
30ml/2 tbsp olive oil
400g/14oz can Puy lentils, rinsed
    and drained
400g/14oz can chopped tomatoes
30ml/2 tbsp chopped fresh flat
    leaf parsley

1 Preheat the oven to 220C/425F/Gas 7. Trim any excess fat from the lamb, and season with salt and pepper.

2 Mix together the breadcrumbs, garlic, herbs and butter or oil, and press on to the fat sides of the lamb. Place in a roasting pan and roast for 25 minutes. Cover with foil; stand for 5 minutes before carving.

3 Cook the onion in the olive oil until softened. Add the lentils and tomatoes and cook gently for 5 minutes, or until the lentils are piping hot. Stir in the parsley and season to taste.

4 Cut each rack of lamb in half and serve with the lentils and new potatoes. Garnish with herb sprigs.

> **Cook's Tips**
> *Your butcher will be happy to prepare the racks of lamb for you if you are unsure of the process. Chining involves removing the backbone from the ribs.*

Roast Leg of Lamb with Rosemary and Garlic

This is a classic combination of flavours, and always popular in the spring lamb season. Serve as a traditional Sunday lunch with roast potatoes and vegetables.

2 garlic cloves, finely sliced
leaves from 2 sprigs of
    fresh rosemary
30ml/2 tbsp olive oil
salt and ground black pepper

Serves 4–6

1 leg of lamb, total weight
    approximately 1.8kg/4lb

1 Preheat the oven to 190°C/375°F/Gas 5. Using a small sharp knife, make slits at 4cm/1½in intervals over the lamb, deep enough to hold a piece of garlic.

2 Push the slices of garlic and the fresh rosemary leaves into the slits in the leg of lamb.

3 Place the lamb in a large roasting pan. Drizzle the olive oil over the top of the lamb and then gently rub it all over the meat with your fingers. Season with plenty of salt and ground black pepper.

4 Place the pan in the preheated oven and roast the lamb for 25 minutes per 450g/1lb of lamb, plus another 25 minutes. The lamb should still be slightly pink in the middle.

5 Remove the lamb from the oven and leave to rest for about 15 minutes before carving.

> **Cook's Tips**
> • *Leaving the lamb to rest before carving gives the meat time to relax after the cooking process and ensures a tender result.*
> • *In addition to roast potatoes and vegetables, you could also serve the classic accompaniment to lamb – mint sauce.*

Herb-crusted Lamb Energy 639kcal/2673kJ; Protein 51.5g; Carbohydrate 28.2g, of which sugars 1.9g; Fat 36.4g, of which saturates 16.7g; Cholesterol 171mg; Calcium 89mg; Fibre 4.9g; Sodium 294mg.
Roast Lamb Energy 518kcal/2177kJ; Protein 61.3g; Carbohydrate 18.1g, of which sugars 1.5g; Fat 22.8g, of which saturates 8.2g; Cholesterol 200mg; Calcium 21mg; Fibre 1.1g; Sodium 138mg.

Rhubarb and Ginger Wine Torte

The springtime harvest of rhubarb provides the opportunity to make this wonderful dessert. The classic combination of rhubarb and ginger is used in this luxury frozen torte to make a dish that is refreshingly tart.

Serves 8
500g/1¼lb rhubarb, trimmed
115g/4oz/generous ½ cup caster
  (superfine) sugar
30ml/2 tbsp water
200g/7oz/scant 1 cup
  cream cheese
150ml/¼ pint/⅔ cups double
  (heavy) cream
40g/1½oz/¼ cup preserved stem
  ginger, finely chopped
a few drops of pink food
  colouring (optional)
250ml/8fl oz/1 cup ginger wine
175g/6oz sponge fingers
fresh mint or lemon balm sprigs,
  dusted with icing (confectioners')
  sugar, to decorate

1 Chop the rhubarb roughly and put it in a pan with the sugar and water. Cover and cook very gently for 5–8 minutes until the rhubarb is just tender. Process in a food processor or blender until smooth, then leave to cool.

2 Beat the cheese in a bowl until softened. Stir in the cream, rhubarb purée and ginger, then food colouring, if you like. Line a 900g/2lb/6–8 cup loaf tin (pan) with clear film (plastic wrap).

3 Pour the mixture into a shallow freezer container and freeze until firm. Alternatively, churn in an ice cream maker.

4 Pour the ginger wine into a shallow dish. Spoon a thin layer of ice cream over the bottom of the tin. Working quickly, dip the sponge fingers in the ginger wine, then lay them lengthways over the ice cream in a single layer, trimming to fit.

5 Spread another layer of ice cream over the top. Repeat the process, adding two to three more layers and finishing with ice cream. Cover and freeze overnight.

6 Transfer to the refrigerator 30 minutes before serving, to soften the torte slightly. To serve, briefly dip in very hot water then invert on to a flat dish. Peel off the lining and decorate.

Ginger and Kiwi Sorbet

Freshly grated root ginger gives a lively, aromatic flavour to this exotic sorbet.

Serves 6
50g/2oz fresh root ginger
115g/4oz/generous ½ cup caster
  (superfine) sugar
300ml/½ pint/1¼ cups water
5 kiwi fruit
fresh mint sprigs or chopped
  kiwi fruit, to decorate

1 Peel the ginger and grate it finely. Put the sugar and water in a pan and heat gently until the sugar has dissolved. Add the ginger and cook for 1 minute, then leave to cool. Strain into a bowl and chill until very cold.

2 Peel the kiwi fruit, place the flesh in a blender and process to form a smooth purée. Add the purée to the chilled syrup and mix well.

3 Pour the kiwi mixture into a freezer container and freeze until slushy. Beat the mixture, then freeze again. Repeat this beating process one more time, then cover the container and freeze until firm.

4 Alternatively, use an ice cream maker. Freeze the mixture following the manufacturer's instructions, then transfer to a freezer container and freeze until required.

5 Remove the sorbet from the freezer 10–15 minutes before serving, to allow it to soften slightly. Spoon into glass bowls, then decorate with mint sprigs or pieces of chopped kiwi fruit and serve immediately.

> **Cook's Tip**
> Fresh ginger root is widely available and is easy to spot with its knobbly shape and pale brown skin. Look for smooth skin and firm solid flesh. Any left over can be wrapped and stored in the refrigerator for up to three weeks. Use a sharp knife for peeling.

Rhubarb Torte Energy 398kcal/1658kJ; Protein 3.9g; Carbohydrate 29.4g, of which sugars 25.2g; Fat 26.8g, of which saturates 16.2g; Cholesterol 100mg; Calcium 132mg; Fibre 1.2g; Sodium 111mg.
Ginger and Kiwi Sorbet Energy 100kcal/426kJ; Protein 0.7g; Carbohydrate 25.3g, of which sugars 25.2g; Fat 0.3g, of which saturates 0g; Cholesterol 0mg; Calcium 23mg; Fibre 1g; Sodium 3mg.

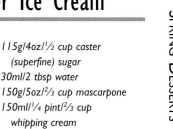

Rhubarb and Ginger Ice Cream

The classic combination of spring rhubarb and root ginger is brought up to date by blending it with mascarpone to make this pretty blush-pink ice cream.

115g/4oz/½ cup caster (superfine) sugar
30ml/2 tbsp water
150g/5oz/⅔ cup mascarpone
150ml/¼ pint/⅔ cup whipping cream
wafer cups, to serve (optional)

Serves 4–6
5 pieces of stem ginger
450g/1lb trimmed rhubarb, sliced

1 Using a sharp knife, roughly chop the stem ginger and set it aside. Put the rhubarb slices into a pan and add the sugar and water. Cover and simmer for 5 minutes until the rhubarb is just tender and still bright pink.

2 Transfer the mixture into a food processor or blender, process until smooth, then leave to cool. Chill if time permits.

3 BY HAND: Mix together the mascarpone, cream and ginger with the rhubarb purée.
USING AN ICE CREAM MAKER: Churn the rhubarb purée for 15–20 minutes until it is thick.

4 BY HAND: Pour the mixture into a plastic tub or similar freezerproof container and freeze for 6 hours or until firm, beating once or twice during the freezing time to break up the ice crystals.
USING AN ICE CREAM MAKER: Put the mascarpone into a bowl, soften it with a wooden spoon, then gradually beat in the cream. Add the chopped ginger, then transfer to the ice cream maker and churn until the ice cream is firm. Serve as scoops in bowls or wafer baskets.

> **Cook's Tip**
> If the rhubarb purée is rather pale, add a few drops of pink colouring when mixing in the cream.

Rhubarb and Raspberry Crumble

A fruit crumble cries out to be eaten on the sofa. It sits beautifully in a bowl, stays where it should – on the spoon and in the mouth – and willingly accepts lashings of cream. The classic fruit to use is rhubarb, preferably the first of the spring when it is bright pink and tender.

Serves 4
675g/1½lb fresh forced rhubarb, cut into large chunks
a pinch of ground allspice
grated rind and juice of 1 lime

175g/6oz/scant 1 cup golden caster (superfine) sugar
225g/8oz fresh or frozen raspberries
custard or clotted cream, to serve

For the crumble
115g/4oz/1 cup plain (all-purpose) flour
pinch of salt
50g/2oz/½ cup ground almonds
115g/4oz/½ cup cold butter
115g/4oz/1 cup blanched almonds, chopped
50g/2oz/¼ cup golden caster (superfine) sugar

1 Preheat the oven to 200°C/400°F/Gas 6 and put a baking sheet inside to heat up. Put the rhubarb in a pan with the allspice, lime rind and juice and sugar. Cook over a gentle heat for 2 minutes, stirring occasionally, until the chunks of rhubarb are tender but still hold their shape.

2 Pour the rhubarb into a sieve (strainer), set over a bowl to catch the juices. Leave to cool. Reserve the juices for later.

3 To make the crumble, put the flour, pinch of salt, ground almonds and butter into a food processor and process until the mixture resembles fine breadcrumbs. Transfer into a bowl and stir in the blanched almonds and sugar.

4 Spoon the rhubarb into a large ovenproof dish, and stir in the raspberries. Sprinkle the almond mixture evenly over the surface, mounding it up a little towards the centre.

5 Place the dish on the baking sheet in the oven and bake for 35 minutes until crisp and golden on top. Cool for 5 minutes before serving with custard or clotted cream and the warmed, reserved rhubarb juices.

Rhubarb Crumble Energy 812kcal/3403kJ; Protein 14.2g; Carbohydrate 88.1g, of which sugars 65.1g; Fat 47.4g, of which saturates 16.9g; Cholesterol 61mg; Calcium 345mg; Fibre 7.7g; Sodium 191mg.
Rhubarb Ice Cream Energy 221kcal/924kJ; Protein 3.6g; Carbohydrate 22.1g, of which sugars 22.1g; Fat 13.8g, of which saturates 8.6g; Cholesterol 37mg; Calcium 94mg; Fibre 1.1g; Sodium 10mg.

Green Devil

Choose a well-flavoured avocado, such as a knobbly, dark-skinned Haas, for this slightly spicy, hot and sour smoothie. Cucumber adds a refreshing edge, while lemon and lime juice zip up the flavour, and the chilli sauce adds an irresistible fiery bite. This is one little devil that is sure to liven up even the most lethargic days.

Serves 2–3
1 small ripe avocado
½ cucumber
30ml/2 tbsp lemon juice
30ml/2 tbsp lime juice
10ml/2 tsp caster (superfine) sugar
pinch of salt
250ml/8fl oz/1 cup apple juice or mineral water
10–20ml/2–4 tsp sweet chilli sauce
ice cubes
red chilli curls, to decorate

1 Halve the avocado and use a sharp knife to remove the stone (pit). Scoop the flesh from both halves into a blender or food processor.

2 Peel and roughly chop the cucumber and add to the blender or food processor, then add the lemon and lime juice, the caster sugar and a little salt.

3 Process the ingredients until smooth and creamy, then add the apple juice or mineral water and a little of the chilli sauce. Blend once more to lightly mix the ingredients together.

4 Pour the smoothie into serving glasses over ice cubes. Decorate with red chilli curls and serve with stirrers and extra chilli sauce.

Cook's Tips
• To make chilli curls, core and seed a fresh red chilli and cut it into very fine strips. Put the strips in a bowl of iced water and leave to stand for 20 minutes or until the strips curl. Use them to decorate this smoothie.
• Seductively smooth avocados are as good for you as they taste. Their fresh vitamin- and mineral-rich flesh is reputed to be fantastic for healthy hair and skin.

Red Alert

This juice is perfect for those times when you're not thinking straight or you need to concentrate. Beetroot, carrots and spinach all contain folic acid, which is known to help maintain a healthy brain, while the addition of fresh orange juice will give your body a natural vitamin boost. This delicious and vibrant blend is guaranteed to set your tastebuds tingling.

Serves 1–2
200g/7oz raw beetroot (beets)
1 carrot
1 large orange
50g/2oz spinach

1 Using a sharp knife, cut the raw beetroot into wedges. Roughly chop the carrot, then cut away the skin from the orange and roughly slice the flesh.

2 Push the orange, beetroot and carrot pieces alternately through a juicer, then add the spinach. Pour into glasses and serve immediately.

Variation
Add piquancy to this drink by stirring in 2.5cm/1 inch-piece of grated fresh root ginger.

Cook's Tips
• Only use fresh, raw, firm beetroot (beet) for juicing, rather than the cooked variety – and most definitely avoid the pickled type that comes in jars. Beetroot juice is a stunning, vibrant red and is surprisingly sweet, especially when mixed with carrot and orange juice.
• Make this drink early in the spring season when beetroot are still available and oranges are plentiful and at their best.

Green Devil Energy 143kcal/598kJ; Protein 1.3g; Carbohydrate 13.2g, of which sugars 12.5g; Fat 9.8g, of which saturates 2.1g; Cholesterol 0mg; Calcium 19mg; Fibre 1.9g; Sodium 6mg.
Red Alert Energy 65kcal/273kJ; Protein 2.8g; Carbohydrate 13.2g, of which sugars 12.4g; Fat 0.5g, of which saturates 0.1g; Cholesterol 0mg; Calcium 75mg; Fibre 1.4g; Sodium 113mg.

Kiwi and Stem Ginger Spritzer

The delicate, refreshingly tangy flavour of kiwi fruit becomes sweeter and more intense when the flesh is juiced. Choose plump, unwrinkled fruits that give a little when gently pressed as under-ripe fruits will produce a slightly bitter taste. A single kiwi fruit contains more than the recommended daily intake of vitamin C, so this juice will boost the system.

Serves 1
2 kiwi fruit
1 piece preserved stem ginger, plus 15ml/1 tbsp syrup from the ginger jar
sparkling mineral water

1 Using a sharp knife, roughly chop the kiwi fruit and the piece of preserved stem ginger. (For a better colour, you may wish to peel the kiwi fruit before chopping, but this is not essential.)

2 Push the pieces of stem ginger and kiwi fruit through a juicer and pour the juice into a large jug (pitcher). Add the ginger syrup and stir to combine.

3 Pour the juice into a tall glass, then top up with plenty of sparkling mineral water and serve immediately.

Variation
If you prefer, you can use still mineral water for this smoothie rather than the sparkling variety, although the added fizz makes the drink more refreshing.

Cook's Tip
Kiwis are a subtropical fruit, not a tropical one, so it is best to store them in the refrigerator before using. If you want them to ripen quickly, store in a closed plastic bag with an apple, pear or banana.

Simply Strawberry

Nothing evokes a sense of wellbeing more than the scent and flavour of sweet, juicy strawberries. By late spring, local berries should be appearing in the stores so grab them while you can.

30–45ml/2–3 tbsp icing (confectioners') sugar
200g/7oz/scant 1 cup Greek (US strained plain) yogurt
60ml/4 tbsp single (light) cream

Serves 2
400g/14oz/3½ cups strawberries, plus extra to decorate

1 Hull the strawberries and place them in a blender or food processor with 30ml/2 tbsp of the icing sugar.

2 Blend to a smooth purée, scraping the mixture down from the side of the bowl with a rubber spatula, if necessary.

3 Add the yogurt and cream and blend again until smooth and frothy.

4 Check the sweetness, adding a little more sugar if you find the flavour too sharp. Pour into glasses and serve decorated with extra strawberries.

Cook's Tip
This recipe uses an abundance of fragrant strawberries so, if possible, make it when the season is right and local ones are at their most plentiful.

Variation
You can replace the strawberries with other fruits if you wish. Try using raspberries, or fresh bananas instead to make another very popular milkshake.

Kiwi Spritzer Energy 104kcal/439kJ; Protein 1.4g; Carbohydrate 24.6g, of which sugars 24.2g; Fat 0.6g, of which saturates 0g; Cholesterol 0mg; Calcium 32mg; Fibre 2.3g; Sodium 45mg.
Simply Strawberry Energy 286kcal/1195kJ; Protein 9.1g; Carbohydrate 30.4g, of which sugars 30.4g; Fat 16.2g, of which saturates 8.9g; Cholesterol 17mg; Calcium 217mg; Fibre 2.2g; Sodium 93mg.

Summer Pea and Chive Soup

This quick and simple soup is light and refreshing. Using fresh garden peas that have just been shelled gives a wonderful flavour to this soup. Simply add them straight to the pan with the hot stock and herbs. Fresh peas are much loved because they are deliciously sweet and tender.

Serves 6
25g/1oz/2 tbsp butter
1 leek, sliced
1 garlic clove, crushed

450g/1lb/4 cups fresh young peas
1.2 litres/2 pints/5 cups vegetable stock
small bunch of fresh chives, coarsely chopped
300ml/½ pint/1¼ cups double (heavy) cream
90ml/6 tbsp Greek (US strained plain) yogurt
4 slices prosciutto, roughly chopped
salt and ground black pepper
fresh chives, to garnish

1 Melt the butter in a pan. Add the leek and garlic, cover and cook gently for 4–5 minutes, until softened. Stir in the fresh peas, stock and chives. Bring slowly to the boil, then simmer for 5 minutes. Cool slightly.

2 Process the soup in a food processor or blender until thick and smooth. Pour into a bowl, stir in the cream and season. Chill for at least 2 hours.

3 Ladle the soup into bowls and add a spoon of Greek yogurt to the centre of each. Sprinkle the chopped prosciutto over the top and garnish with chives before serving.

Cook's Tips
• Use kitchen scissors to trim and cut prosciutto – for best results do this straight into the soup, so that the pieces fall neatly rather than sticking together.
• For a clever garnish, cut five lengths of chives to about 6cm/2½in, then use another chive to tie them together. Lay this on top of the soup.

Chilled Cucumber and Prawn Soup

If you've never served a chilled soup before, this is the perfect one to try. Delicious, attractive and light, it's the perfect way to celebrate summer.

Serves 4
25g/1oz/2 tbsp butter
2 shallots, finely chopped
2 garlic cloves, crushed
1 cucumber, peeled, seeded and diced
300ml/½ pint/1¼ cups milk

225g/8oz/2 cups cooked peeled prawns (shrimp)
15ml/1 tbsp each finely chopped fresh mint, dill, chives and chervil
300ml/½ pint/1¼ cups whipping cream
salt and ground white pepper

For the garnish
30ml/2 tbsp crème fraîche (optional)
4 large, cooked prawns (shrimp), peeled with tail intact
fresh dill and chives

1 Melt the butter in a pan and cook the shallots and garlic over a low heat until soft but not coloured. Add the cucumber and cook gently, stirring frequently, until tender.

2 Stir in the milk, bring almost to boiling point, then lower the heat and simmer for 5 minutes. Transfer the soup into a blender or food processor and process until very smooth. Season the soup to taste with salt and ground white pepper.

3 Pour the soup into a large bowl and leave to cool. When cool, stir in the prawns, chopped herbs and cream. Cover, transfer to the refrigerator and chill for at least 2 hours.

4 To serve, ladle the soup into individual bowls, top each portion with a spoonful of crème fraîche, if using, and place a prawn over the edge of each dish. Sprinkle a little extra dill over each bowl and tuck two or three chives under the prawns on the edge of the bowls to garnish. Serve immediately.

Cook's Tip
If you prefer hot soup, reheat it gently until hot but not boiling. Do not boil, or the delicate flavour will be spoilt.

Summer Pea Soup Energy 386kcal/1610kJ; Protein 20.6g; Carbohydrate 32.8g, of which sugars 4.5g; Fat 20.1g, of which saturates 6.9g; Cholesterol 53mg; Calcium 47mg; Fibre 5.3g; Sodium 682mg.
Cucumber Soup Energy 439kcal/1817kJ; Protein 18.9g; Carbohydrate 7.5g, of which sugars 7.1g; Fat 37.2g, of which saturates 23.1g; Cholesterol 255mg; Calcium 212mg; Fibre 0.5g; Sodium 245mg.

Vichyssoise

This classic, chilled potato soup was first created in the 1920s by Louis Diat, chef at the New York Ritz-Carlton. He named it after Vichy, near his home in France.

Serves 4–6
50g/2oz/¼ cup unsalted butter
450g/1lb leeks, white parts only, thinly sliced
3 large shallots, sliced
250g/9oz floury potatoes (such as King Edward or Maris Piper), peeled and cut into chunks
1 litre/1¾ pints/4 cups light chicken stock or water
300ml/½ pint/1¼ cups double (heavy) cream
iced water (optional)
a little lemon juice (optional)
salt and ground black pepper
chopped fresh chives, to garnish

1 Melt the butter in a heavy pan and cook the leeks and shallots gently, covered, for about 15–20 minutes, until soft but not browned.

2 Add the potatoes and cook, uncovered, for a few minutes. Stir in the stock or water with 5ml/1 tsp salt and pepper to taste. Bring to the boil, then reduce the heat and partly cover the pan. Simmer for 15 minutes, or until the potatoes are soft.

3 Cool, then process the mixture until smooth in a blender or food processor. Strain the soup into a bowl and stir in the cream. Taste and adjust the seasoning and add a little iced water if the consistency of the soup seems too thick.

4 Chill the soup for at least 4 hours or until very cold. Before serving taste the chilled soup for seasoning and add a squeeze of lemon juice, if required. Pour the soup into bowls and sprinkle with chopped chives. Serve immediately.

Variations
• Add about 50g/2oz/1 cup shredded sorrel to the soup at the end of cooking. Finish and chill as in the main recipe, then serve the soup garnished with a little pile of finely shredded sorrel.
• The same amount of watercress can be used in the same way.

Yogurt Soup with Chilli Salsa

The refreshing flavours of cucumber and yogurt in this soup fuse with the cool salsa and the smoky flavour of the charred salmon topping to bring a taste of summer to the table.

Serves 4
3 medium cucumbers
300ml/½ pint/1¼ cups Greek (US strained plain) yogurt
250ml/8fl oz/1 cup vegetable stock, chilled
120ml/4fl oz/½ cup crème fraîche
15ml/1 tbsp chopped fresh chervil
15ml/1 tbsp chopped fresh chives
15ml/1 tbsp chopped fresh flat leaf parsley
1 small red chilli, seeded and very finely chopped
a little oil, for brushing
225g/8oz salmon fillet, skinned and cut into eight thin slices
salt and ground black pepper
fresh chervil or chives, to garnish

1 Peel two of the cucumbers and halve them lengthways. Scoop out and discard the seeds, then roughly chop the flesh. Purée in a food processor or blender, then add the yogurt, stock, crème fraîche, chervil, chives and seasoning, and process until smooth. Chill.

2 Peel, halve and seed the remaining cucumber. Cut the flesh into small neat dice. Mix with the chopped parsley and chilli. Chill until required.

3 Brush a griddle or frying pan with oil and heat until very hot. Sear the salmon slices for 1–2 minutes on each side, until tender and charred.

4 Ladle the chilled soup into soup bowls. Top with two slices of the salmon, then pile a portion of salsa into the centre of each. Garnish with the chervil or chives and serve.

Variation
• Fresh tuna can be used instead of salmon.
• For a vegetarian alternative, make this soup with brown halved cherry tomatoes and diced halloumi cheese.

Vichyssoise Energy 547Kcal/2260kJ; Protein 4.6g; Carbohydrate 17.7g, of which sugars 6.8g; Fat 51.4g, of which saturates 31.7g; Cholesterol 129mg; Calcium 79mg; Fibre 3.6g; Sodium 103mg.
Yogurt Soup Energy 226Kcal/942kJ; Protein 15.8g; Carbohydrate 9.1g, of which sugars 5.9g; Fat 14.4g, of which saturates 2.3g; Cholesterol 29mg; Calcium 177mg; Fibre 0.6g; Sodium 91mg.

Griddled Tomatoes on Soda Bread

Nothing could be simpler than this summer brunch dish, transformed into something special by adding a drizzle of olive oil, balsamic vinegar and shavings of Parmesan cheese to griddled tomatoes and serving them on toast.

Serves 4
olive oil, for brushing and drizzling
6 tomatoes, thickly sliced
4 thick slices soda bread
balsamic vinegar, for drizzling
salt and ground black pepper
shavings of Parmesan cheese,
 to serve

1 Brush a griddle pan with olive oil and heat over high heat. Add the tomato slices and cook for about 4–6 minutes, turning once, until softened and slightly blackened on both sides. Alternatively, heat a grill (broiler) to high and line the rack with foil. Grill (broil) the tomato slices for about 4–6 minutes, turning once, until softened.

2 While the tomatoes are cooking, lightly toast the soda bread. Place the tomatoes on top of the toast and drizzle each portion with a little olive oil and vinegar. Season to taste and serve immediately with thin shavings of Parmesan.

Tapenade and Quail's Eggs

Tapenade is a purée made from capers, olives and anchovies. It is popularly used in Mediterranean cooking. It complements the taste of eggs perfectly, especially quail's eggs, which look very pretty on open sandwiches.

45ml/3 tbsp tapenade
curly endive leaves
3 small tomatoes, sliced
black olives
4 canned anchovy fillets, drained
 and halved lengthways
parsley sprigs, to garnish

Serves 8
8 quail's eggs
1 small baguette

1 Boil the quail's eggs for 3 minutes, then plunge them straight into cold water to cool. Crack the shells gently and remove them very carefully.

2 Cut the baguette into slices on the diagonal and spread each one with some of the tapenade.

3 Arrange a little curly endive, torn to fit, and the tomato slices on top of the tapenade.

4 Halve the quail's eggs and place them on top of the tomato slices. Finish with a little more tapenade, the olives and finally the anchovies. Garnish with small parsley sprigs.

Variation
A dish like this one tastes perfect on its own, but if you prefer something more substantial, add slices of bacon, grilled (broiled) until crisp, or some herby sausage. When cooking the sausage, don't prick it first, as this allows juices to flow out and tends to make the sausage dry. If you grill (broil) the sausage under low to medium heat, and turn it often, it will be unlikely to burst.

Cook's Tip
Using a griddle pan reduces the amount of oil required for cooking the tomatoes and gives them a barbecued flavour. The ridges on the pan brand the tomatoes, which gives them an attractive appearance.

Cook's Tip
To make 300ml/½ pint/1¼ cups of tuna tapenade, put a 90g/3½oz canned drained tuna in a food processor with 25g/1oz/2 tbsp capers, 10 canned anchovy fillets and 75g/3oz/¾ cup pitted black olives and blend until smooth, scraping down the sides as necessary. Gradually add 60ml/ 4 tbsp olive oil through the feeder tube. This purée can be used for filling hard-boiled eggs. Blend the tapenade with the egg yolks then pile into the whites.

Tapenade and Eggs Energy 157kcal/666kJ; Protein 6.3g; Carbohydrate 28.4g, of which sugars 1.8g; Fat 2.8g, of which saturates 0.6g; Cholesterol 37mg; Calcium 76mg; Fibre 1.5g; Sodium 523mg.
Griddled Tomatoes Energy 178kcal/751kJ; Protein 4.2g; Carbohydrate 26.3g, of which sugars 6.9g; Fat 7g, of which saturates 1g; Cholesterol 0mg; Calcium 66mg; Fibre 2.7g; Sodium 175mg.

Courgette Fritters with Chilli Jam

Chilli jam is hot, sweet and sticky – rather like a thick chutney. It adds a delicious piquancy to these light courgette fritters which are always a popular summertime snack.

Makes 12
450g/1lb/3½ cups coarsely
    grated courgettes (zucchini)
50g/2oz/⅔ cup freshly grated
    Parmesan cheese

2 eggs, beaten
60ml/4 tbsp plain
    (all-purpose) flour
vegetable oil, for frying
salt and ground black pepper

For the chilli jam
75ml/5 tbsp olive oil
4 large onions, diced
4 garlic cloves, chopped
1–2 green chillies, seeded
    and sliced
30ml/2 tbsp soft dark brown sugar

1 First make the chilli jam. Heat the oil in a frying pan until hot, then add the onions and the garlic. Cook for 20 minutes, stirring frequently, until the onions are very soft.

2 Leave the onion mixture to cool, then transfer to a food processor or blender. Add the chillies and sugar and blend until smooth, then return the mixture to the pan. Cook for a further 10 minutes, stirring frequently, until the liquid evaporates and the mixture has the consistency of jam. Cool slightly.

3 To make the fritters, squeeze the courgettes in a dish towel to remove any excess liquid, then combine with the Parmesan, eggs, flour and salt and pepper.

4 Heat enough oil to cover the base of a large frying pan. Add 30ml/2 tbsp of the mixture for each fritter and cook three fritters at a time. Cook for 2–3 minutes on each side until golden, then keep warm while you cook the rest. Drain on kitchen paper and serve warm with a spoonful of the chilli jam.

> **Cook's Tip**
> *Stored in an airtight jar in the refrigerator, the chilli jam will keep for up to 1 week.*

Tomato and Courgette Timbales

Timbales are baked savoury custards, mainly made with light vegetables. This combination is delicious as a summery appetizer. It can be served warm or cool. Try other combinations if you like and choose different herbs as well.

Serves 4
a little butter
2 courgettes (zucchini),
    about 175g/6oz

2 firm, ripe vine tomatoes, sliced
2 eggs plus 2 egg yolks
45ml/3 tbsp double
    (heavy) cream
15ml/1 tbsp fresh tomato
    sauce or passata (bottled
    strained tomatoes)
10ml/2 tsp chopped fresh basil or
    oregano or 5ml/1 tsp dried
salt and ground black pepper
salad leaves, to serve

1 Preheat the oven to 180°C/350°F/Gas 4. Lightly butter four large ramekins. Top and tail the courgettes, then cut them into thin slices.

2 Place the courgette slices into a steamer and steam over a pan of boiling water for 4–5 minutes. Drain well in a colander, then layer the courgettes in the ramekins, alternating with the sliced tomatoes.

3 In a large mixing bowl, whisk together the eggs, cream, tomato sauce or passata, herbs and seasoning. Pour the egg mixture into the ramekins.

4 Place the ramekins in a roasting pan and half fill with hot water. Bake for 20–30 minutes until the custard is just firm.

5 Cool slightly, then run a knife round the rims and carefully turn out on to small plates. Serve with salad leaves.

> **Cook's Tip**
> *Don't overcook the timbales or the texture of the savoury custard will become rubbery.*

Courgette Fritters Energy 157kcal/652kJ; Protein 4.4g; Carbohydrate 11.1g, of which sugars 6.1g; Fat 10.8g, of which saturates 2.2g; Cholesterol 36mg; Calcium 85mg; Fibre 1.2g; Sodium 59mg.
Tomato Timbales Energy 72kcal/299kJ; Protein 5.1g; Carbohydrate 2.7g, of which sugars 2.5g; Fat 4.7g, of which saturates 1.3g; Cholesterol 146mg; Calcium 35mg; Fibre 1g; Sodium 55mg.

Summer Salad with Capers and Olives

Make this tasty salad in the summer when tomatoes are at their sweetest and full of flavour. Serve with warm ciabatta or walnut bread.

Serves 4

4 tomatoes
½ cucumber
1 bunch spring onions (scallions), trimmed and chopped
1 bunch watercress
8 stuffed olives
30ml/2 tbsp drained capers

For the dressing
30ml/2 tbsp red wine vinegar
5ml/1 tsp paprika
2.5ml/½ tsp ground cumin
1 garlic clove, crushed
75ml/5 tbsp extra virgin olive oil
salt and ground black pepper

1 Using a sharp knife, make a small cross on the top of the tomatoes, then plunge into a bowl of boiling water for about 1–2 minutes. Peel off the skin, then finely dice the flesh. Place in a salad bowl.

2 Peel the cucumber, dice finely and add to the tomatoes. Add half the spring onions to the salad bowl and mix lightly.

3 Break the watercress into sprigs. Add them to the tomato mixture, with the olives and capers and mix well.

4 To make the dressing, mix the wine vinegar, paprika, cumin and garlic in a bowl. Whisk in the oil and add salt and black pepper to taste.

5 Pour the dressing over the salad and toss lightly. Serve immediately with the remaining spring onions.

Variation
If you cannot find any watercress, you can use other leaves in its place. Rocket (arugula) has a similar peppery taste and texture to watercress and is therefore ideal as a substitute in this recipe.

Cucumber and Tomato Salad with Yogurt Dressing

Luxurious Greek yogurt, olive oil and sweet summer tomatoes combine deliciously in this recipe.

Serves 4

450g/1lb firm ripe tomatoes
½ cucumber
1 onion
1 small fresh red or green chilli, seeded and chopped, or fresh chives, chopped into 2.5cm/1in lengths, to garnish
crusty bread or pitta breads, to serve

For the dressing
60ml/4 tbsp olive or vegetable oil
90ml/6 tbsp Greek (US strained plain) yogurt
30ml/2 tbsp chopped fresh parsley or chives
2.5ml/½ tsp vinegar
salt and ground black pepper

1 Cut a small cross in the bottom of each tomato and plunge them into a pan of boiling water for about 1 minute, then transfer them to a bowl of cold water. Drain, then slip off and discard their skins. Halve the tomatoes, remove and discard the seeds and cores and chop the flesh into even pieces. Put them into a salad bowl.

2 Chop the cucumber and onion into pieces of a similar size to the tomatoes and put them in the bowl.

3 Mix all the dressing ingredients together and season to taste. Pour the dressing over the salad and toss all the ingredients together thoroughly.

4 Season with black pepper and garnish with the chilli or chives. Serve with crusty bread or pile into pitta pockets.

Cook's Tip
If you have time, before assembling the salad salt the chopped cucumber lightly and leave it in a colander for 30 minutes to drain. This will avoid making the salad watery.

Summer Salad Energy 172kcal/712kJ; Protein 2.5g; Carbohydrate 5g, of which sugars 4.3g; Fat 16g, of which saturates 2.4g; Cholesterol 0mg; Calcium 71mg; Fibre 2.2g; Sodium 305mg.
Cucumber Salad Energy 156kcal/646kJ; Protein 3g; Carbohydrate 5.8g, of which sugars 5.4g; Fat 13.9g, of which saturates 2.9g; Cholesterol 0mg; Calcium 75mg; Fibre 2.1g; Sodium 32mg.

Tomato Salad with Marinated Peppers and Oregano

This refreshing appetizer is perfect for when tomatoes are at their best in summer with maximum flavour and sweetness. They combine superbly with marinated peppers, which, because they have been well roasted before soaking, are sweeter and more digestible than raw ones.

Serves 4–6

2 marinated (bell)
  peppers, drained
6 ripe tomatoes, sliced
15ml/1 tbsp chopped
  fresh oregano
75ml/5 tbsp olive oil
30ml/2 tbsp white wine vinegar
sea salt

1 If the marinated peppers are in large pieces, cut them into even strips. Arrange the tomato slices and pepper strips on a serving dish, sprinkle with the fresh oregano and season to taste with sea salt.

2 Whisk together the olive oil and white wine vinegar in a jug (pitcher) and pour the dressing over the salad. Serve the salad immediately or cover the dish and chill in the refrigerator until required.

Cook's Tips
• *Marinated (bell) peppers are widely available in jars, often labelled as pimentos. However, they are much tastier when prepared yourself. To do this, wrap one green and one red pepper in foil and place on a baking sheet. Cook in a preheated oven at 180°C/350°F/Gas 4, or under a preheated grill (broiler), turning occasionally, for 20–30 minutes, until tender. Unwrap and when cool, peel the peppers, then halve and seed. Cut the flesh into strips and pack into a screw-top jar. Add olive oil to cover, close and store in the refrigerator for up to 6 days.*
• *You can preserve marinated peppers by cooking them in a closed jar in boiling water for about 30 minutes. They can then be kept for approximately 6 weeks.*

Tomato and Mozzarella Salad

Sweet, naturally ripened tomatoes and fresh basil leaves capture the essence of summer in this simple Mediterranean salad. Choose ripe plum or beefsteak tomatoes for this dish – whatever is available at the grocery store.

Serves 4

5 ripe tomatoes
2 x 225g/8oz buffalo mozzarella
  cheese, drained
1 small red onion, chopped

For the dressing
½ small garlic clove, peeled

15g/½ oz/½ cup fresh
  basil leaves
30ml/2 tbsp chopped fresh flat
  leaf parsley
25ml/1½ tbsp small salted
  capers, rinsed
2.5ml/½ tsp mustard
75–90ml/5–6 tbsp extra virgin
  olive oil
5–10ml/1–2 tsp balsamic vinegar
ground black pepper

For the garnish
fresh basil leaves
fresh parsley sprigs

1 First make the dressing. Put the garlic, basil, parsley, half the capers and the mustard in a food processor or blender and process briefly to chop.

2 Then, with the motor running, gradually pour in the olive oil through the feeder tube to make a smooth purée with a dressing consistency.

3 Add the balsamic vinegar to the dressing to taste. Season with plenty of ground black pepper.

4 Slice the tomatoes and the mozzarella. Arrange the tomato and cheese slices alternately on a serving plate. Sprinkle the chopped red onion over the top and season with a little ground black pepper.

5 Drizzle the dressing over the salad, then sprinkle a few basil leaves, parsley sprigs and the remaining capers over the top as a garnish. Set aside and leave for about 10–15 minutes before serving.

Tomato Salad Energy 119kcal/494kJ; Protein 1.4g; Carbohydrate 6.9g, of which sugars 6.7g; Fat 9.7g, of which saturates 1.5g; Cholesterol 0mg; Calcium 17mg; Fibre 2.1g; Sodium 12mg.
Tomato and Mozzarella Energy 261kcal/1080kJ; Protein 11.2g; Carbohydrate 3.1g, of which sugars 3.1g; Fat 22.7g, of which saturates 9.4g; Cholesterol 33mg; Calcium 211mg; Fibre 1g; Sodium 231mg.

Onion Tart

This tart also makes a delicious main course when served warm with a fresh, summery salad.

Serves 4–6

175g/6oz/1½ cups plain
   (all-purpose) flour
75g/3oz/6 tbsp butter, chilled
30–45ml/2–3 tbsp iced water

For the filling
50g/2oz/¼ cup butter
900g/2lb Spanish (Bermuda)
   onions, thinly sliced
1 egg plus 2 egg yolks
250ml/8fl oz/1 cup double
   (heavy) cream
1.5ml/¼ tsp freshly grated nutmeg
salt and ground black pepper

1 Process the flour, a pinch of salt and the chilled butter in a food processor until reduced to fine crumbs. Add the iced water and process briefly to form a dough. Wrap in clear film (plastic wrap) and chill for 40 minutes.

2 For the filling, melt the butter in a pan and add the onions and a pinch of salt. Turn them in the butter. Cover and cook very gently, stirring frequently, for 30–40 minutes. Cool slightly.

3 Preheat the oven to 190°C/375°F/Gas 5. Roll out the dough thinly and use to line a 23–25cm/9–10in loose-based flan tin (pan). Line with foil or baking parchment and baking beans, then bake blind for 10 minutes.

4 Remove the foil or parchment and baking beans, and bake for another 4–5 minutes, until the pastry is lightly cooked to a pale brown colour (blonde is a good description). Reduce the oven temperature to 180°C/350°F/Gas 4.

5 Beat the egg, egg yolks and cream together. Season with salt, lots of black pepper and the grated nutmeg. Place half the onions in the pastry shell and add half the egg mixture. Add the remaining onions, then pour in as much of the remaining custard as you can.

6 Place on a baking sheet and bake on the middle shelf for 40–50 minutes, or until the custard is risen, browned and set in the centre. Serve warm rather than piping hot.

Tomato and Black Olive Tart

This delicious tart has a fresh, rich Mediterranean flavour and is perfect for summer picnics. If you are taking this tart on a picnic, use a rectangular tin, which makes it easier to transport and cut into portions at the picnic destination.

3 eggs, beaten
300ml/½ pint/1¼ cups milk
30ml/2 tbsp chopped fresh herbs,
   such as parsley, marjoram
   or basil
6 firm plum tomatoes
75g/3oz ripe Brie cheese
about 16 black olives, pitted
salt and ground black pepper

Serves 8
375g/13oz shortcrust pastry, at
   room temperature

1 Preheat the oven to 190°C/375°F/Gas 5. Roll out the pastry thinly on a lightly floured surface. Line a 28 × 18cm/11 × 7in loose-based rectangular flan tin (pan), trimming off any overhanging edges.

2 Line the pastry case (pie shell) with baking parchment and baking beans, and bake blind for 15 minutes. Remove the baking parchment and beans and bake for a further 5 minutes until the base is crisp.

3 Meanwhile, mix together the eggs, milk, seasoning and herbs. Slice the tomatoes, cube the cheese, and slice the olives. Place the prepared flan case on a baking sheet, arrange the tomatoes, cheese and olives in the bottom of the case, then pour in the egg mixture. Transfer carefully to the oven and bake for about 40 minutes until just firm and turning golden. Slice hot or cool in the tin, then serve.

Variations
• This tart is delicious made with other cheeses. Try slices of Gorgonzola or Camembert for a slightly stronger flavour.
• Alternatively, sprinkle a few strips of anchovy fillet over the tart before baking.

Onion Tart Energy 548kcal/2271kJ; Protein 7.4g; Carbohydrate 35.4g, of which sugars 9.7g; Fat 42.9g, of which saturates 25.6g; Cholesterol 200mg; Calcium 115mg; Fibre 3g; Sodium 156mg.
Tomato and Olive Tart Energy 315kcal/1316kJ; Protein 9.3g; Carbohydrate 26.1g, of which sugars 4.6g; Fat 19.9g, of which saturates 7.2g; Cholesterol 90mg; Calcium 151mg; Fibre 1.7g; Sodium 505mg.

Baked Tomatoes with Mint

This is a dish for the height of the summer when the tomatoes are falling off the vines and are very ripe, juicy and full of flavour. Mint flourishes in sunny or shady places, as well as growing well in pots. This tomato dish goes especially well with lamb.

Serves 4
6 large ripe tomatoes
300ml/¹⁄₂ pint/1¹⁄₄ cups double (heavy) cream
2 sprigs of fresh mint
olive oil, for brushing
a few pinches of caster (superfine) sugar
30ml/2 tbsp grated Bonnet cheese
salt and ground black pepper

1 Preheat the oven to 220°C/425°F/Gas 7. Bring a pan of water to the boil and have a bowl of iced water ready. Cut the cores out of the tomatoes and make a cross at the base. Plunge the tomatoes into the boiling water for 10 seconds and then straight into the iced water. Leave to cool completely.

2 Put the cream and mint in a small pan and bring to the boil. Reduce the heat and allow to simmer until it has reduced by about half.

3 When the tomatoes have cooled enough to handle, peel and slice them thinly.

4 Brush a shallow gratin dish lightly with a little olive oil. Layer the sliced tomatoes in the dish, overlapping slightly, and season with salt and ground black pepper. Sprinkle a little sugar over the top.

5 Strain the reduced cream evenly over the top of the tomatoes. Sprinkle on the cheese and bake in the preheated oven for 15 minutes, or until the top is browned and bubbling. Serve immediately in the gratin dish.

> **Cook's Tip**
> Bonnet is a hard goat's cheese but any hard, well-flavoured cheese will do.

Rocket and Tomato Pizza

Peppery rocket and aromatic basil add both colour and lots of summery flavour to this crisp pizza.

Serves 2
10ml/2 tsp olive oil, plus extra for drizzling
1 garlic clove, crushed
150g/5oz/1 cup canned chopped tomatoes
2.5ml/¹⁄₂ tsp sugar
30ml/2 tbsp torn fresh basil leaves
2 tomatoes, seeded and chopped

150g/5oz/²⁄₃ cup mozzarella cheese, sliced
20g/³⁄₄oz/1 cup rocket (arugula) leaves
rock salt and ground black pepper

For the pizza base
225g/8oz/2 cups strong white flour, sifted
5ml/1 tsp salt
2.5ml/¹⁄₂ tsp easy-blend (rapid-rise) dried yeast
15ml/1 tbsp olive oil

1 To make the pizza base, place the flour, salt and yeast in a bowl. Add the oil and 150ml/¹⁄₄ pint/²⁄₃ cup warm water to a well in the centre. Mix to form a soft dough.

2 Turn out the dough on to a floured work surface and knead for 5 minutes. Cover with the upturned bowl or a dish towel and leave for 5 minutes. Knead for a further 5 minutes until the dough is smooth and elastic. Place in an oiled bowl and cover. Leave in a warm place for 45 minutes until doubled in bulk.

3 Preheat the oven to 220°C/425°F/Gas 7. Make the topping. Heat the oil in a frying pan and fry the garlic for 1 minute. Add the tomatoes and sugar, and cook for 5–7 minutes until thickened. Stir in the basil and seasoning, then set aside.

4 Knead the risen dough lightly, then roll out to form a rough 30cm/12in round. Place on a lightly oiled baking sheet and push up the edges of the dough to form a shallow, even rim.

5 Spoon the tomato mixture over the base, then top with fresh tomatoes. Arrange the mozzarella on top. Season with rock salt and pepper and drizzle with a little olive oil. Bake in the top of the oven for 10–12 minutes until crisp and golden. Sprinkle the rocket over the pizza just before serving.

Grilled Vegetable Pizza

You really can't go too far wrong with this classic mixture of Mediterranean grilled vegetables on home-made pizza dough. It is filling and healthy, and is a favourite in summer.

Serves 6

1 courgette (zucchini), sliced
2 baby aubergines (eggplants) or
  1 small aubergine, sliced
30ml/2 tbsp olive oil
1 yellow (bell) pepper, seeded
  and sliced

115g/4oz/1 cup cornmeal
50g/2oz/½ cup potato flour
50g/2oz/½ cup soya flour
5ml/1 tsp baking powder
2.5ml/½ tsp sea salt
50g/2oz/¼ cup non-
  hydrogenated margarine
about 105ml/7 tbsp milk
4 plum tomatoes, skinned
  and chopped
30ml/2 tbsp chopped fresh basil
115g/4oz buffalo mozzarella
  cheese, sliced
sea salt and ground black pepper
fresh basil sprigs, to garnish

1 Preheat the grill (broiler). Brush the courgette and aubergine slices with a little oil and place on a grill rack with the pepper slices. Cook under the grill until lightly browned, turning once.

2 Meanwhile, preheat the oven to 200°C/400°F/Gas 6. Place the cornmeal, potato flour, soya flour, baking powder and salt in a mixing bowl and stir to mix. Lightly rub in the margarine until the mixture resembles coarse breadcrumbs, then stir in enough of the milk to make a soft but not sticky dough.

3 Place the pizza dough on a sheet of baking parchment on a baking sheet and roll or gently press it out to form a 25cm/10in round, making the edges slightly thicker than the centre.

4 Lightly brush the pizza dough with any remaining oil, then spread the chopped plum tomatoes evenly over the dough.

5 Sprinkle with the basil and seasoning. Arrange the grilled (broiled) vegetables over the tomatoes and top with the cheese.

6 Bake for about 25–30 minutes until crisp and golden brown. Garnish the pizza with fresh basil sprigs and serve immediately, cut into slices.

Conchiglie with Roasted Vegetables

Nothing could be simpler – or more delicious – than tossing freshly cooked pasta with roasted summer vegetables. The flavour is absolutely superb.

Serves 4–6

1 red (bell) pepper, seeded and
  cut into 1cm/½in squares
1 yellow or orange (bell) pepper,
  seeded and cut into
  1cm/½in squares
1 small aubergine (eggplant),
  roughly diced

2 courgettes (zucchini),
  roughly diced
75ml/5 tbsp extra virgin olive oil
15ml/1 tbsp chopped fresh
  flat leaf parsley
5ml/1 tsp dried oregano
  or marjoram
250g/9oz baby Italian plum
  tomatoes, hulled and
  halved lengthways
2 garlic cloves, roughly chopped
350–400g/12–14oz/3–3½ cups
  dried conchiglie
salt and ground black pepper
4–6 fresh marjoram or oregano
  flowers, to garnish

1 Preheat the oven to 190°C/375°F/Gas 5. Rinse the prepared peppers, aubergine and courgettes in a sieve (strainer) or colander under cold running water, drain, then transfer the vegetables into a large roasting pan.

2 Pour about 45ml/3 tbsp of the olive oil over the vegetables and sprinkle with the fresh and dried herbs. Add salt and pepper to taste and stir well.

3 Roast the vegetables in the preheated oven for about 30 minutes, stirring two or three times during the cooking.

4 Stir the tomatoes and garlic into the vegetable mixture, then roast for 20 minutes more, stirring once or twice.

5 Meanwhile, cook the pasta according to the instructions on the packet. Drain the pasta and transfer it into a warmed bowl.

6 Add the roasted vegetables and the remaining oil to the pasta and toss well. Serve the pasta and vegetables hot in warmed individual bowls, sprinkling each portion with a few herb flowers.

Vegetable Pizza Energy 400kcal/1666kJ; Protein 11.9g; Carbohydrate 34.6g, of which sugars 9.6g; Fat 23.9g, of which saturates 5.3g; Cholesterol 18mg; Calcium 166mg; Fibre 4.4g; Sodium 240mg.
Conchiglie with Vegetables Energy 277kcal/1171kJ; Protein 9.5g; Carbohydrate 50.3g, of which sugars 8.7g; Fat 5.5g, of which saturates 0.8g; Cholesterol 0mg; Calcium 52mg; Fibre 4.6g; Sodium 11mg.

Sweet Romanos Stuffed with Two Cheeses and Cherry Peppers

Romanos are wonderful Mediterranean peppers. They are long, pointy and slightly gnarled, and look a little like a large poblano chilli. Not hot but delightfully sweet, their flavour is nicely balanced by the ricotta salata.

Serves 4
4 sweet romano peppers,
    preferably in mixed colours,
    total weight about 350g/12oz
90ml/6 tbsp extra virgin olive oil
200g/7oz mozzarella cheese
10 drained bottled sweet cherry
    peppers, finely chopped
115g/4oz ricotta salata
30ml/2 tbsp chopped fresh
    oregano leaves
24 black olives
2 garlic cloves, crushed
salt and ground black pepper
dressed mixed salad leaves and
    bread, to serve

1 Prepare the barbecue. Split the peppers lengthways and remove the seeds and membrane. Rub 15ml/1 tbsp of the oil all over the peppers. Place them hollow-side uppermost.

2 Slice the mozzarella and divide equally among the pepper halves. Sprinkle over the chopped cherry peppers, season lightly and crumble the ricotta salata over the top, followed by the oregano leaves and olives. Mix the garlic with the remaining oil and add a little salt and pepper. Spoon about half the mixture over the filling in the peppers.

3 Once the flames have died down, rake the coals to one side. Position a lightly oiled grill rack over the coals to heat. When the coals are medium-hot, or with a moderate coating of ash, place the filled peppers on the section of grill rack that is not over the coals. Cover with a lid, or improvise with a wok lid or tented heavy-duty foil. Grill for 6 minutes.

4 Spoon the remaining oil mixture over the filling, replace the lid and continue to grill for 6–8 minutes more, or until the peppers are lightly charred and the cheese has melted. Serve the peppers immediately with a dressed green or leafy salad and bread.

Roasted Vegetable Quesadillas with Melted Mozzarella

Barbecuing gives these vegetables a wonderful smoky flavour, enhanced by the bite of green chillies.

Serves 4
8 long baby aubergines
    (eggplants), total weight about
    175g/6oz, halved lengthways
2 red onions, cut into wedges,
    leaving the roots intact
2 red (bell) peppers, quartered
1 yellow and 1 orange (bell)
    pepper, quartered
30ml/2 tbsp olive oil
400g/14oz block
    mozzarella cheese
2 fresh green chillies, seeded and
    sliced into rounds
15ml/1 tbsp tomato sauce
8 corn or wheat flour tortillas
handful of fresh basil leaves
salt and ground black pepper

1 Toss the aubergines, onions and peppers in the oil on a large baking sheet. Place the peppers, skin side down, on the griddle or directly on the grill rack of a medium hot barbecue and cook until seared and browned underneath. If the food starts to char, remove the rack until the coals cool down.

2 Put the peppers in a bowl, cover with clear film (plastic wrap) and set aside. Grill (broil) the onions and aubergines until they have softened slightly and are branded with brown grill marks, then set aside. Rub the skins off the peppers with your fingers, cut each piece in half and add to the other vegetables.

3 Cut the mozzarella into 20 slices. Place them, together with the roasted vegetables, in a large bowl and add the sliced chillies and the tomato sauce. Stir well to mix, and season with salt and pepper.

4 Place a griddle over the heat. When it is hot, lay a tortilla on the griddle and pile a quarter of the vegetable mixture into the centre. Sprinkle over some basil leaves. When the tortilla has browned underneath, put another tortilla on top, cooked side down. Turn the quesadilla over and continue to cook until the underside has browned. Keep warm while you cook the remaining quesadillas. Serve immediately.

Vegetable Quesadillas Energy 233kcal/971kJ; Protein 11.8g; Carbohydrate 17.1g, of which sugars 8.5g; Fat 13.6g, of which saturates 7.4g; Cholesterol 29mg; Calcium 214mg; Fibre 2.7g; Sodium 268mg.
Sweet Romanos Energy 95kcal/399kJ; Protein 5.6g; Carbohydrate 12.8g, of which sugars 12g; Fat 2.8g, of which saturates 0.7g; Cholesterol 48mg; Calcium 53mg; Fibre 4.5g; Sodium 301mg.

Farfalle with Courgettes and Prawns

In this modern recipe, pink prawns and green courgettes combine prettily with cream and pasta bows to make a substantial main course for summer. Serve with crusty Italian rolls or warm ciabatta bread.

Serves 4

50g/2oz/¼ cup butter
2–3 spring onions (scallions), very
  thinly sliced on the diagonal
350g/12oz courgettes (zucchini),
  thinly sliced on the diagonal
60ml/4 tbsp dry white wine
300g/11oz/2¾ cups
  dried farfalle
75ml/5 tbsp crème fraîche
225g/8oz/1⅓ cups peeled
  cooked prawns (shrimp),
  thawed and thoroughly dried
  if frozen
15ml/1 tbsp finely chopped fresh
  marjoram or flat leaf parsley, or
  a mixture
salt and ground black pepper

1 Melt the butter in a large pan, add the spring onions and cook over a low heat, stirring frequently, for about 5 minutes until softened. Add the courgettes, with salt and pepper to taste, and stir-fry for 5 minutes. Pour over the wine and let it bubble, then cover and simmer for 10 minutes.

2 Cook the pasta in a pan of salted boiling water according to the instructions on the packet. Meanwhile, add the crème fraîche to the courgette mixture and simmer for about 10 minutes until well reduced.

3 Add the prawns to the courgette mixture, heat through gently and taste for seasoning. Drain the pasta and transfer it into a warmed bowl. Add the sauce and chopped herbs and toss well. Serve immediately.

Variation
Use penne instead of the farfalle, and asparagus tips instead of the courgettes (zucchini), if you like.

Light and Fragrant Tiger Prawns with Cucumber and Dill

This simple, elegant dish has a fresh, light flavour full of the tastes of summer. It is equally good for a simple supper or a dinner party.

Serves 4

500g/1¼lb raw tiger prawns
  (jumbo shrimp), peeled with
  tail on
500g/1¼lb cucumber
30ml/2 tbsp butter
15ml/1 tbsp olive oil
15ml/1 tbsp finely chopped garlic
45ml/3 tbsp chopped fresh dill
juice of 1 lemon
salt and ground black pepper
steamed rice or noodles, to serve

1 Using a small, sharp knife, carefully make a shallow slit along the back of each prawn and use the point of the knife to remove the black vein. Set the prawns aside.

2 Peel the cucumber and slice in half lengthways. Using a small teaspoon, gently scoop out all the seeds and discard. Cut the cucumber into 4 × 1cm/1½ × ½in sticks.

3 Heat a wok over a high heat, then add the butter and oil. When the butter has melted, add the cucumber and garlic and stir-fry over a high heat for 2–3 minutes.

4 Add the prepared prawns to the wok and continue to stir-fry over a high heat for 3–4 minutes, or until the prawns turn pink and are just cooked through, then remove from the heat.

5 Add the fresh dill and lemon juice to the wok and toss to combine. Season well with salt and ground black pepper and serve immediately with steamed rice or noodles.

Variation
The delicate flavour of prawns (shrimp) goes really well with cucumber and fragrant dill, but if you prefer a more robust dish, toss in a handful of chives as well.

Farfalle Energy 490kcal/2058kJ; Protein 21.1g; Carbohydrate 57.9g, of which sugars 4.7g; Fat 19.8g, of which saturates 11.9g; Cholesterol 158mg; Calcium 102mg; Fibre 3.1g; Sodium 191mg.
Fragrant Prawns Energy 165kcal/691kJ; Protein 15.7g; Carbohydrate 10.5g, of which sugars 10.1g; Fat 7g, of which saturates 0.9g; Cholesterol 171mg; Calcium 78mg; Fibre 0.3g; Sodium 167mg.

Fried Eel with Creamy Potatoes

This dish is a great way to enjoy fried eel. Served with these delicious potatoes and accompanied by a cold beer, this seasonal dish is a summer speciality.

Serves 4
about 1kg/2¼lb eel, skinned
    and cleaned
1 egg
5ml/1 tsp water
25g/1oz/½ cup fine
    breadcrumbs, toasted
10ml/2 tsp salt
2.5ml/½ tsp white pepper

40g/1½oz/3 tbsp butter
2 lemons, sliced into wedges,
    to garnish

For the potatoes
800g/1¾lb potatoes, peeled
5ml/1 tsp salt
40g/1½oz/3 tbsp butter
20g/¾oz/4 tbsp plain
    (all-purpose) flour
475ml/16fl oz/2 cups single
    (light) cream
salt and white pepper, to taste
45ml/3 tbsp chopped fresh
    parsley, to garnish

1 Using a sharp knife, cut the skinned eel into 10cm/4in lengths. Whisk together the egg and water in a shallow dish. Place the breadcrumbs in a second shallow dish. Dip the eel first into the egg mixture, then into the breadcrumbs to coat both sides evenly. Sprinkle with salt and pepper. Leave the fish aside to rest for at least 10 minutes.

2 Melt the butter in a large pan over medium-high heat. Add the eel pieces and cook, turning once, for around 10 minutes on each side, depending on thickness, until the coating is golden brown and the eel is tender. Remove from the pan and drain on kitchen paper. Keep warm.

3 Meanwhile, boil the potatoes in salted water for about 20 minutes. Drain, slice and keep warm. Melt the butter in a pan and stir in the flour. Cook, stirring, for 5 minutes until the roux is pale beige. Slowly stir in the cream and cook for about 5 minutes, stirring constantly, until the sauce has thickened. Season to taste.

4 Stir the potato slices into the cream sauce. Serve with the fried eel on warmed plates, garnished with the parsley, lemon wedges and accompanied by fresh vegetables, if you wish.

Salted and Grilled Sardines

Grilled sardines are classic Mediterranean beach food. Nothing beats grilling these fresh fish on a barbecue at the coast on a hot summer's day. Serve with focaccia or fresh crusty bread.

Serves 4–8
8 sardines, about 800g/1¾lb
    total weight, scaled and gutted
50g/2oz/¼ cup salt
oil, for brushing

focaccia or fresh crusty bread,
    to serve (optional)

For the herb salsa
5ml/1 tsp sea salt flakes
60ml/4 tbsp chopped fresh
    tarragon leaves
40g/1½oz/generous 1 cup
    chopped flat leaf parsley
1 small red onion, very
    finely chopped
105ml/7 tbsp extra virgin olive oil
60ml/4 tbsp lemon juice

1 Make the herb salsa by grinding the salt in a mortar and adding the other salsa ingredients one at a time.

2 Wash the sardines inside and out. Pat dry with kitchen paper and rub them inside and out with salt. Cover and put in a cool place for 30–45 minutes. Meanwhile, prepare the barbecue.

3 Rinse the salt off the sardines. Pat them dry with kitchen paper, then leave to air-dry for 15 minutes.

4 When the coals have a thick coating of ash, brush the fish with olive oil and cook directly on the oiled grill.

5 Cook the fish for about 3 minutes on one side and about 2½ minutes on the other. Serve immediately with the herb salsa and bread.

Cook's Tip
Fresh sardines are only available for a very limited season during the summer months, usually close to where they have been caught. Sardine is a slightly generic term for young, small fish – usually it refers to young pilchards but canned sardines may be sprats or herring as well.

Fried Eel Energy 978kcal/4074kJ; Protein 50.2g; Carbohydrate 43.7g, of which sugars 5.6g; Fat 68.2g, of which saturates 32.3g; Cholesterol 483mg; Calcium 184mg; Fibre 2.3g; Sodium 448mg.
Salted Sardines Energy 423kcal/1,754kJ; Protein 31.5g; Carbohydrate 1.8g, of which sugars 1.4g; Fat 32.1g, of which saturates 6.4g; Cholesterol 0mg; Calcium 187mg; Fibre 1g; Sodium 667mg.

Plaice Fillets with Sorrel and Lemon Butter

Sorrel is a wild herb that is now grown commercially. It is very good in salads and, roughly chopped, it partners this slightly sweet-fleshed fish very well. Plaice – such a pretty fish with its orange spots and fern-like frills – is a delicate fish that works well with this sauce. Cook the fish simply like this to get the full natural flavours of the ingredients.

Serves 4
200g/7oz/scant 1 cup butter
500g/1¼lb plaice fillets, skinned
  and patted dry
30ml/2 tbsp chopped
  fresh sorrel
90ml/6 tbsp dry white wine
a little lemon juice

1 Heat half the butter in a large frying pan and, just as it is melted, place the fillets skin side down. Cook briefly, just to firm up, reduce the heat and turn the fish over. The fish will be cooked in less than 5 minutes. Try not to let the butter brown or allow the fish to colour.

2 Carefully remove the fish fillets from the pan with a metal spatula and keep them warm between two plates. Cut the remaining butter into chunks.

3 Add the chopped sorrel to the pan and stir. Add the wine, then, as it bubbles, add the butter, swirling it in piece by piece and not allowing the sauce to boil. Stir in a little lemon juice.

4 Serve the fish with the sorrel and lemon butter spooned over, with some crunchy green beans and perhaps some new potatoes, if you like.

> **Variation**
> *Instead of using sorrel, you could try this recipe with fresh tarragon or thyme.*

Fried Plaice with Tomato and Basil Sauce

This simple summer dish is perennially popular with children. It works equally well with lemon sole or dabs (these do not need skinning), or fillets of haddock and whiting.

Serves 4
25g/1oz/¼ cup plain
  (all-purpose) flour
2 eggs, beaten
75g/3oz/¾ cup dried
  breadcrumbs, preferably
  home-made

4 small plaice or flounder, skinned
15g/½oz/1 tbsp butter
15ml/1 tbsp sunflower oil
salt and ground black pepper
1 lemon, quartered, to serve
fresh basil leaves, to garnish

For the tomato sauce
30ml/2 tbsp olive oil
1 red onion, finely chopped
1 garlic clove, finely chopped
400g/14oz can chopped tomatoes
15ml/1 tbsp tomato purée (paste)
15ml/1 tbsp torn fresh basil leaves

1 First make the tomato sauce. Heat the olive oil in a large pan, add the finely chopped onion and garlic and cook gently for about 5 minutes, until softened and pale golden. Stir in the chopped tomatoes and tomato purée and simmer for 20–30 minutes, stirring occasionally. Season with salt and pepper and stir in the basil.

2 Spread out the flour in a shallow dish, pour the beaten eggs into another and spread out the breadcrumbs in a third. Season the fish with salt and pepper.

3 Hold a fish in your left hand and dip it first in flour, then in egg and finally, in the breadcrumbs, patting the crumbs on with your dry right hand.

4 Heat the butter and oil in a frying pan until foaming. Fry the fish one at a time in the hot fat for about 5 minutes on each side, until golden brown and cooked through, but still juicy in the middle. Drain on kitchen paper and keep hot while you fry the rest. Serve with lemon wedges and the tomato sauce, garnished with basil leaves.

Plaice Fillets Energy 494kcal/2047kJ; Protein 25.7g; Carbohydrate 0.5g, of which sugars 0.5g; Fat 43.3g, of which saturates 26.4g; Cholesterol 170mg; Calcium 98mg; Fibre 0.3g; Sodium 501mg.
Fried Plaice Energy 333kcal/1390kJ; Protein 22.5g; Carbohydrate 14.2g, of which sugars 3.9g; Fat 21.1g, of which saturates 2.5g; Cholesterol 0mg; Calcium 90mg; Fibre 1.3g; Sodium 279mg.

Baked Cod with Beer and Lemon

Cod is one of the most popular types of fish, as it has a mild flavour and plenty of dense, meaty white flesh that can be cooked in a variety of ways during its peak season in the summer.

Serves 4
90g/3½oz/7 tbsp butter
1 small onion or 3 shallots, very finely chopped
handful of chopped fresh parsley
drizzle of vegetable oil or olive oil
4 cod fillets, each about 175g/6oz
1 bay leaf
300ml/½ pint/1¼ cups white beer, such as Hoegaarden, or dry white wine
8 lemon slices
4 thyme sprigs
60ml/4 tbsp soft white breadcrumbs
chopped fresh parsley and lemon wedges, to garnish
boiled or steamed potatoes, to serve

1 Preheat the oven to 180°C/350°F/Gas 4. Using half the butter, grease a flameproof casserole. Add the onion or shallots and parsley. Drizzle with the oil. Transfer the casserole to the oven and cook the onion for about 4 minutes.

2 Season the cod fillets on both sides. Place on top of the onion and parsley mix. Add the bay leaf and pour in the beer or wine to almost cover the fish. Top each fillet with two lemon slices and a thyme sprig.

3 Return the casserole to the oven and bake for 15–20 minutes, depending on the thickness of the fillets, until the fish flakes when tested with the tip of a sharp knife. Transfer the fillets to a platter, cover with foil and keep warm.

4 Put the casserole over medium heat on top of the stove. Cook for 4–5 minutes until the juices have reduced by about three quarters. Add the breadcrumbs and stir until they have been absorbed.

5 Cut the remaining butter into small cubes and add to the sauce, a little at a time. Stir until thick and creamy. If is too thick, add more beer or wine to thin it. Check the seasoning and pour the sauce over the fish. Garnish with the parsley and lemon wedges, and serve with the potatoes.

Marinated Sea Trout

Sea trout has a superb texture and a flavour like that of wild salmon. It is best served with strong but complementary flavours, such as chillies and lime, that cut the richness of its flesh.

Serves 6
6 sea trout cutlets, each about 115g/4oz, or wild or farmed salmon
2 garlic cloves, chopped
1 fresh long red chilli, seeded and chopped
45ml/3 tbsp chopped Thai basil
15ml/1 tbsp sugar or palm sugar (jaggery)
3 limes
400ml/14fl oz/1⅔ cups coconut milk
15ml/1 tbsp fish sauce

1 Place the sea trout or salmon cutlets side by side in a shallow dish. Using a pestle, pound the chopped garlic and chilli in a large mortar to break them both up roughly. Add about 30ml/2 tbsp of the Thai basil with the sugar and continue to pound to a rough paste.

2 Grate the rind from 1 lime and squeeze the juice. Mix the rind and juice into the chilli paste, with the coconut milk. Pour the mixture over the cutlets. Cover and chill for about 1 hour. Cut the remaining limes into wedges.

3 Take the fish out of the refrigerator so that it can return to room temperature. Remove the cutlets from the marinade. Either cook on a barbecue, in an oiled hinged wire fish basket, or under a hot grill (broiler). Cook the fish for 4 minutes on each side, trying not to move them. They may stick to the grill rack if not seared first.

4 Strain the remaining marinade into a pan, reserving the contents of the sieve (strainer). Bring the marinade to the boil, then simmer gently for 5 minutes, stirring. Stir in the contents of the sieve and continue to simmer for 1 minute more. Add the fish sauce and the remaining Thai basil.

5 Lift each fish cutlet on to a warmed serving plate, pour over the sauce and serve immediately with the lime wedges.

Baked Cod Energy 407kcal/1695kJ; Protein 27.5g; Carbohydrate 13g, of which sugars 1.4g; Fat 25.3g, of which saturates 12.5g; Cholesterol 111mg; Calcium 44mg; Fibre 0.6g; Sodium 339mg.
Marinated Sea Trout Energy 157kcal/662kJ; Protein 23.1g; Carbohydrate 5.9g, of which sugars 5.9g; Fat 4.7g, of which saturates 0.1g; Cholesterol 0mg; Calcium 46mg; Fibre 0.4g; Sodium 141mg.

Spatchcock Poussins with Herbes de Provence Butter

Spatchcock is said to be a distortion of an 18th-century Irish expression 'dispatch cock' for providing an unexpected guest with a quick and simple meal. A young summer chicken was prepared without frills or fuss by being split, flattened and fried or grilled.

Serves 2
2 poussins, each weighing about 450g/1lb
1 shallot, finely chopped
2 garlic cloves, crushed
45ml/3 tbsp chopped mixed fresh herbs, such as flat leaf parsley, sage, rosemary and thyme
75g/3oz/6 tbsp butter, softened
salt and ground black pepper

1 To spatchcock a poussin, place it breast down on a chopping board and split it along the back. Open out the bird and turn it over, so that the breast side is uppermost.

2 Press the poussin as flat as possible on to the chopping board, then thread two metal skewers through it, across the breast and thigh, to keep it flat.

3 Repeat the spatchcocking process with the second poussin. Place the skewered birds on a large grill (broiler) pan.

4 Place the chopped shallot, crushed garlic and chopped mixed herbs in a large bowl. Add the butter with plenty of seasoning, and then beat until well combined. Dot the butter over the spatchcock poussins.

5 Preheat the grill to high and cook the poussins for about 30 minutes, turning them over halfway through. Turn again and baste with the cooking juices, then cook for a further 5–7 minutes on each side. Serve immediately.

Variation
Add some finely chopped chilli or a little grated lemon rind to the butter.

Pandanus-flavoured Chicken Satay with Hot Cashew Nut Sambal

Pandanus leaves are frequently used in South-east Asian cooking, in both savoury and sweet dishes. They are very versatile, and in this recipe they give the chicken a delicate flavour.

Serves 6
about 1kg/2¼lb skinless chicken breast fillets
30ml/2 tbsp olive oil
5ml/1 tsp ground coriander
2.5ml/½ tsp ground cumin
2.5cm/1in piece fresh root ginger, finely grated
2 garlic cloves, crushed

5ml/1 tsp caster (superfine) sugar
2.5ml/½ tsp salt
18 long pandanus leaves, each halved to give 20cm/8in lengths
36 bamboo or wooden skewers

For the cashew nut sambal
2 garlic cloves, roughly chopped
4 small fresh hot green chillies (not tiny birdseye chillies), seeded and sliced
50g/2oz/⅓ cup cashew nuts
10ml/2 tsp sugar, preferably palm sugar (jaggery)
75ml/5 tbsp light soy sauce
juice of ½ lime
30ml/2 tbsp coconut cream

1 To make the sambal, place the garlic and chillies in a mortar and grind them quite finely with a pestle. Add the nuts and continue to grind until the mixture is almost smooth, with just a bit of texture. Pound in the remaining ingredients, cover and leave in a cool place until needed.

2 Soak the skewers in water for 30 minutes. Slice the chicken horizontally into thin pieces and then into strips about 2.5cm/1in wide. Toss in the oil. Mix the coriander, cumin, ginger, garlic, sugar and salt together. Rub this mixture into the strips of chicken. Leave to marinate while you prepare the barbecue.

3 Thread a strip of leaf and a piece of chicken lengthways on to each skewer. Position an oiled grill rack over the coals to heat.

4 Cook over medium-hot coals, meat-side down, covered with a lid or tented heavy-duty foil for 5–7 minutes. Once the meat has seared, move the satays around so that the leaves don't scorch. Serve hot, with the sambal.

Poussins Energy 621kcal/2583kJ; Protein 50.1g; Carbohydrate 0.3g, of which sugars 0.3g; Fat 46.8g, of which saturates 16.4g; Cholesterol 288mg; Calcium 21mg; Fibre 0g; Sodium 256mg.
Pandanus Chicken Energy 197kcal/835kJ; Protein 42.5g; Carbohydrate 2.4g, of which sugars 2g; Fat 2g, of which saturates 0.5g; Cholesterol 123mg; Calcium 15mg; Fibre 0.4g; Sodium 640mg.

Grilled Skewered Chicken

These fabulous little skewers, cooked on the barbecue, make the ideal finger food for a summer's day gathering.

Serves 4
8 chicken thighs with skin, boned
8 large, thick spring onions
   (scallions), trimmed

oil, for greasing
lemon wedges, to serve

For the yakitori sauce
60ml/4 tbsp sake
75ml/5 tbsp shoyu
15ml/1 tbsp mirin
15ml/1 tbsp unrefined caster
   (superfine) sugar

1 First, make the yakitori sauce. Mix all the ingredients together in a small pan. Bring to the boil, then reduce the heat and simmer for 10 minutes.

2 Cut the chicken into 2.5cm/1in cubes. Cut the spring onions into 2.5cm/1in long sticks. To cook the chicken on a barbecue, soak eight bamboo skewers overnight in water. This prevents the skewers from burning during cooking. Prepare the barbecue. Thread about four pieces of chicken and three spring onion pieces on to each of the skewers. Place the yakitori sauce in a small bowl and have a brush ready.

3 Cook the skewered chicken on the barbecue. Keep the skewer handles away from the fire, turning them frequently. Brush the chicken with sauce. Return to the coals and repeat this process twice more until the chicken is well cooked.

4 Alternatively, to grill (broil), preheat the grill (broiler) to high. Oil the wire rack and spread out the chicken cubes on it. Grill both sides of the chicken until the juices drip, then dip the pieces in the sauce and put back on the rack. Grill for 30 seconds on each side, repeating the dipping process twice more.

5 Set aside and keep warm. Gently grill the spring onions until soft and slightly brown outside. Do not dip. Thread the chicken and spring onion pieces on to skewers as above. Arrange the skewered chicken and spring onions on a serving platter and serve accompanied by lemon wedges.

Tandoori Drumsticks with Kachumbar

This classic tandoori dish can be barbecued, if the weather permits, or baked in the oven. Kachumbar, a cool salad laced with chillies, is a perfect accompaniment. Use sweet white onions if you can't find pink ones.

Serves 6
12 skinless chicken drumsticks
3 garlic cloves, crushed to a paste
   with a pinch of salt
150ml/1/4 pint/2/3 cup strained
   natural (plain) yogurt
10ml/2 tsp ground coriander
5ml/1 tsp ground cumin
5ml/1 tsp ground turmeric
1.5ml/1/4 tsp cayenne pepper

2.5ml/1/2 tsp garam masala
15ml/1 tbsp curry paste
juice of 1/2 lemon
salt
warmed naan breads, to serve

For the kachumbar
2 pink onions, halved and
   thinly sliced
10ml/2 tsp salt
4cm/11/2in piece of fresh root
   ginger, finely shredded
2 fresh long green chillies, seeded
   and finely chopped
20ml/4 tsp sugar, preferably palm
   sugar (jaggery)
juice of 1/2 lemon
60ml/4 tbsp chopped fresh
   coriander (cilantro)

1 Place the drumsticks in a non-metallic bowl. Put the garlic, yogurt, spices, curry paste and lemon juice in a food processor and whizz until smooth. Pour the mixture over the drumsticks to coat, cover and chill overnight.

2 Two hours before serving, make the kachumbar. Put the onion slices in a bowl, sprinkle them with the salt, cover and leave to stand for 1 hour. Transfer into a sieve (strainer), rinse well under cold running water, then drain and pat dry. Roughly chop the slices and put them in a serving bowl. Add the remaining ingredients and mix well. About 30 minutes before cooking, drain the drumsticks in a sieve set over a bowl.

3 Prepare the barbecue, if using, or preheat the oven to 190°C/375°F/Gas 5. Salt the drumsticks, wrap the tips with strips of foil to prevent them from burning, then place on the grill rack so that they are not directly over the coals. Cover with a lid or tented heavy-duty foil and grill or roast for 15–20 minutes, turning. Serve with the kachumbar and naan bread.

Skewered Chicken Energy 165kcal/695kJ; Protein 22g; Carbohydrate 9g, of which sugars 8.8g; Fat 2.9g, of which saturates 0.8g; Cholesterol 105mg; Calcium 24mg; Fibre 0.4g; Sodium 1429mg.
Tandoori Drumsticks Energy 423kcal/1771kJ; Protein 30g; Carbohydrate 58g, of which sugars 8.5g; Fat 7.8g, of which saturates 0.7g; Cholesterol 70mg; Calcium 63mg; Fibre 1.2g; Sodium 1210mg.

Beef Meatballs in a Tomato and Wine Sauce

These tasty meatballs in tomato sauce are usually served in tapas bars in individual casserole dishes, accompanied by crusty bread. They make a good summer supper, too, with a green salad or pasta.

Serves 4
225g/8oz minced (ground) beef
4 spring onions (scallions), thinly sliced

2 garlic cloves, finely chopped
30ml/2 tbsp grated Parmesan cheese
10ml/2 tsp fresh thyme leaves
15ml/1 tbsp olive oil
3 tomatoes, chopped
30ml/2 tbsp red or dry white wine
10ml/2 tsp chopped fresh rosemary
pinch of sugar
salt and ground black pepper
fresh thyme, to garnish

1 Put the minced beef in a bowl. Add the spring onions, garlic, Parmesan and thyme and plenty of salt and pepper. Stir the mixture well to combine. Using your hands, shape the mixture into 12 small firm meatballs.

2 Heat the olive oil in a large, heavy frying pan and cook the meatballs for 5–8 minutes, turning often, until evenly browned.

3 Add the chopped tomatoes, wine, rosemary and sugar to the pan, with salt and ground black pepper to taste.

4 Cover the pan and cook gently for about 15 minutes until the tomatoes are pulpy and the meatballs are cooked through. Check the sauce for seasoning and serve the meatballs hot, garnished with the thyme.

Variation
If you prefer to make larger beefburgers, shape the meat mixture into four wide patties and fry. Serve the patties on a slice of grilled (broiled) beefsteak tomato, or surrounded by tomato sauce. Top with a fried egg, if you like.

Polpettes with Mozzarella and Tomato

These Italian meatballs are made with beef and topped with slices of mozzarella cheese and tomato.

Serves 6
½ slice white bread, crusts removed
45ml/3 tbsp milk
675g/1½lb minced (ground) beef
1 egg, beaten

50g/2oz/½ cup dry breadcrumbs
vegetable oil for frying
2 beefsteak or other large tomatoes, sliced
15ml/1 tbsp chopped fresh oregano
1 mozzarella cheese, cut into 6 slices
6 drained canned anchovies, cut in half lengthways
salt and ground black pepper

1 Preheat the oven to 200°C/400°F/Gas 6. Put the bread and milk into a small pan and heat very gently, until the bread absorbs all the milk.

2 Mash the soaked bread to a pulp with a fork or potato masher. Set aside to cool.

3 Put the minced beef into a large bowl with the bread mixture and the egg. Season with salt and black pepper. Mix well, then shape the mixture into six patties.

4 Sprinkle the breadcrumbs on to a plate and dredge the patties, coating them thoroughly.

5 Heat about 5mm/¼in oil in a large frying pan. Add the patties and fry for 2 minutes on each side, until brown. Transfer to a greased ovenproof dish, in a single layer.

6 Lay a slice of tomato on top of each patty, sprinkle with oregano and season with salt and pepper. Place the mozzarella slices on top. Arrange two strips of anchovy, placed in a cross on top of each slice of mozzarella.

7 Bake for about 10–15 minutes, until the mozzarella has melted. Serve hot, straight from the dish.

Meatballs Energy 206kcal/857kJ; Protein 14.7g; Carbohydrate 2.5g, of which sugars 2.5g; Fat 14.6g, of which saturates 5.9g; Cholesterol 41mg; Calcium 105mg; Fibre 0.9g; Sodium 135mg.
Polpettes Energy 230kcal/960kJ; Protein 8.4g; Carbohydrate 20.9g, of which sugars 2.3g; Fat 13.1g, of which saturates 5.3g; Cholesterol 68mg; Calcium 122mg; Fibre 1.4g; Sodium 446mg.

Spicy Beefburgers

The coconut used in these burgers, which may seem an unusual ingredient, gives them a rich and succulent flavour. They taste wonderful accompanied by a sharp yet sweet mango chutney and can be eaten in mini naan or pitta breads.

Serves 8

500g/1¼lb/2½ cups minced (ground) beef
5ml/1 tsp anchovy paste
10ml/2 tsp tomato purée (paste)
10ml/2 tsp ground coriander
5ml/1 tsp ground cumin
7.5ml/1½ tsp finely grated fresh root ginger
2 garlic cloves, crushed
1 egg white
75g/3oz solid creamed coconut or 40g/1½oz desiccated (dry unsweetened shredded) coconut
45ml/3 tbsp chopped fresh coriander (cilantro)
salt and ground black pepper
8 fresh vine leaves (optional), to serve
mango chutney and mini naan or pitta breads, to serve

1 Mix the minced beef, anchovy paste, tomato purée, coriander, cumin, ginger and garlic in a bowl. Add the egg white, with salt and pepper to taste. Using your hands, mix well.

2 Grate the block of coconut and work it gently into the meat mixture so that it doesn't melt, with the fresh coriander. Form the mixture into eight burgers, about 7.5cm/3in in diameter. Chill for 30 minutes.

3 Prepare the barbecue. Once the flames have died down, rake the hot coals to one side and insert a drip tray flat beside them. Position a lightly oiled grill rack over the coals to heat.

4 When the coals are medium-hot, or with a moderate coating of ash, place the chilled burgers on the rack over the drip tray. Cook for 10–15 minutes, turning them over once or twice. Check that they are cooked by breaking off a piece of one of the burgers.

5 If you are using vine leaves, wash them and pat dry with kitchen paper. Wrap one around each burger. Serve with mango chutney and mini naan or pitta breads.

Steak Ciabatta with Hummus

This family favourite tastes all the better when enjoyed on a sunny beach after a day spent battling the surf.

Serves 4

3 garlic cloves, crushed to a paste with enough salt to season the steaks
30ml/2 tbsp extra virgin olive oil
4 sirloin steaks, 2.5cm/1in thick, total weight about 900g/2lb
2 romaine lettuce hearts
4 small ciabatta breads, split
salt and ground black pepper

For the dressing
10ml/2 tsp Dijon mustard
5ml/1 tsp cider or white wine vinegar
15ml/1 tbsp olive oil

For the hummus
400g/14oz can chickpeas, drained and rinsed
45ml/3 tbsp tahini
2 garlic cloves, crushed
juice of 1 lemon
30ml/2 tbsp water
60ml/4 tbsp extra virgin olive oil

1 To make the hummus, process the chickpeas in a food processor to form a paste. Add the tahini, garlic, lemon juice and seasoning. Pour in the water and pulse to mix. Scrape into a jar and pour the oil over. Cover, then put in a cool place.

2 Make a dressing for the salad by mixing the mustard and vinegar in a small jar. Gradually whisk in the oil, then season.

3 Mix the crushed garlic and oil together in a shallow dish. Add the steaks and rub the mixture into both surfaces. Cover and leave in a cool place until ready to cook.

4 Prepare the barbecue. Once the flames have died down, position a lightly oiled grill rack over the coals to heat. When the coals are ready, cook the steaks. For rare steaks, cook for 2 minutes on one side, then 3 minutes on the other. Medium steaks will take 4 minutes each side. Leave to rest for 2 minutes.

5 Separate and dress the romaine leaves. Place the ciabatta cut side down on the rack for a minute. Spread the hummus, with any oil, on the bottom half of each ciabatta. Slice the steaks and arrange on top of the hummus, with some of the leaves. Replace the lids and cut each filled ciabatta in half to serve.

Spicy Burgers Energy 177kcal/734kJ; Protein 13.4g; Carbohydrate 0.8g, of which sugars 0.7g; Fat 13.4g, of which saturates 7g; Cholesterol 38mg; Calcium 22mg; Fibre 1.1g; Sodium 90mg.
Steak Ciabatta Energy 765kcal/3210kJ; Protein 69.8g; Carbohydrate 55.2g, of which sugars 2.8g; Fat 30.8g, of which saturates 7.4g; Cholesterol 115mg; Calcium 222mg; Fibre 6.7g; Sodium 783mg.

Blueberry and Vanilla Crumble

In this heavenly dessert, vanilla ice cream is packed into a buttery crumble case with summer berries and baked until the ice cream melts over the crumble.

Serves 8
225g/8oz/2 cups plain
  (all-purpose) flour
5ml/1 tsp baking powder
175g/6oz/³⁄4 cup unsalted
  butter, diced
150g/5oz/³⁄4 cup caster
  (superfine) sugar
1 egg
75g/3oz/³⁄4 cup ground almonds
10ml/2 tsp natural vanilla extract
5ml/1 tsp ground mixed spice
500ml/17fl oz/2¼ cups vanilla
  ice cream
175g/6oz/1½ cups blueberries
icing (confectioners') sugar,
  for dusting

1 Preheat the oven to 180°C/350°F/Gas 4. Put the flour and baking powder in a food processor. Add the butter and process briefly to mix. Add the sugar and process briefly again until the mixture is crumbly. Remove about 175g/6oz/1½ cups of the crumble mixture and set this aside.

2 Add the egg, ground almonds, vanilla extract and mixed spice to the remaining crumble mixture and blend to a paste. Scrape the paste into a 20cm/8in springform tin (pan). Press it firmly on to the base and halfway up the sides to make an even case. Line the case with baking parchment and fill with baking beans.

3 Sprinkle the crumble mixture on to a baking sheet. Bake the crumble for 20 minutes and the case for 30 minutes until pale golden. Remove the paper and beans and bake the case for 5 minutes. Leave both the crumble and the case to cool.

4 Pack the ice cream into the almond pastry case and level the surface. Sprinkle with the blueberries and then the baked crumble mixture. Freeze overnight.

5 About 25 minutes before serving, preheat the oven to 180°C/350°F/Gas 4. Bake the crumble for 10–15 minutes, until the ice cream has started to soften. Dust with icing sugar and serve in wedges.

Strawberry Cream Shortbreads

Simple to assemble, these pretty strawberry desserts are always popular in the summer season. Serve them as soon as they are ready because the shortbread biscuits will lose their lovely crisp texture if left to stand for too long.

Serves 3
150g/5oz/generous 1 cup
  strawberries
450ml/³⁄4 pint/scant 2 cups
  double (heavy) cream
6 round shortbread biscuits
fresh mint sprigs, to
  decorate (optional)

1 Reserve three strawberries for decoration. Hull the remaining strawberries and cut them in half.

2 Put the halved strawberries in a bowl and gently crush using the back of a fork. (Only crush the berries lightly; they should not be reduced to a purée.)

3 Put the cream in a large, clean bowl and whip to form soft peaks. Add the crushed strawberries and gently fold in to combine – do not overmix.

4 Halve the reserved strawberries, then spoon the strawberry and cream mixture on top of the shortbread biscuits. Decorate each one with half a strawberry and a mint sprig, if you like. Serve immediately.

Cook's Tip
Use whole strawberries for the decoration and give them a pretty frosted effect by painting with whisked egg white, then dipping in caster (superfine) sugar. Leave to dry before serving.

Variation
You can use any other berry you like for this dessert – try raspberries or blueberries. Two ripe, peeled peaches will also give great results.

Strawberry Shortbreads Energy 890kcal/3673kJ; Protein 4.4g; Carbohydrate 22g, of which sugars 9.6g; Fat 87.8g, of which saturates 54.8g; Cholesterol 225mg; Calcium 105mg; Fibre 1g; Sodium 106mg.
Blueberry Crumble Energy 522kcal/2183kJ; Protein 8.1g; Carbohydrate 57.7g, of which sugars 34.4g; Fat 29.7g, of which saturates 15.9g; Cholesterol 86mg; Calcium 142mg; Fibre 2g; Sodium 182mg.

Chocolate Redcurrant Torte

A sumptuously rich cake that will be the centrepiece of any summer table.

Serves 8–10
115g/4oz/¹/₂ cup unsalted
   (sweet) butter, softened
115g/4oz/¹/₂ cup dark
   muscovado (molasses) sugar
2 eggs
150ml/¹/₄ pint/²/₃ cup sour cream
150g/5oz/1¹/₄ cups self-raising
   (self-rising) flour
5ml/1 tsp baking powder

50g/2oz/¹/₂ cup unsweetened
   cocoa powder
75g/3oz/³/₄ cup stemmed
   redcurrants, plus 115g/4oz/1 cup
   redcurrant sprigs, to decorate

For the icing
150g/5oz plain (semisweet)
   chocolate, chopped into
   small pieces
45ml/3 tbsp redcurrant jelly
30ml/2 tbsp dark rum
120ml/4fl oz/¹/₂ cup double
   (heavy) cream

1 Preheat the oven to 180°C/350°F/Gas 4. Grease a 1.2 litre/ 2 pint/5 cup ring tin (pan) and dust lightly with flour. Cream the butter with the sugar in a mixing bowl until pale and fluffy. Beat in the eggs and sour cream until thoroughly mixed.

2 Sift the flour, baking powder and cocoa over the mixture, then fold in evenly. Fold in the stemmed redcurrants. Spoon into the tin and level the surface. Bake for 40–50 minutes, or until well risen. Turn out on to a wire rack to cool completely.

3 Make the icing. Mix the chocolate, redcurrant jelly and rum in a heatproof bowl over a pan of simmering water. Stir until melted. Remove from the heat and cool to room temperature, then add the cream, stirring until the mixture is well blended.

4 Transfer the cake to a serving plate. Spoon the icing over, drizzling it down the sides. Decorate with redcurrant sprigs.

Cook's Tip
Use a decorative gugelhupf tin, if you have one. Add a little cocoa powder to the flour used for dusting the greased tin, as this will prevent the cake from being streaked with white.

Summer Pudding

Unbelievably simple to make and totally delicious, this is a real warm-weather classic featuring mixed summer fruits. It's also a productive way of using up any leftover bread you may have.

Serves 4
about 8 slices white bread, at
   least one day old
800g/1³/₄lb mixed summer fruits
about 25g/1oz/2 tbsp sugar
30ml/2 tbsp water

1 Remove the crusts from the bread. Cut a round from one slice of bread to fit in the base of a 1.2 litre/2 pint/5 cup round ovenproof bowl and place in position. Cut strips of bread about 5cm/2in wide and use to line the sides of the bowl, overlapping the strips as you work.

2 Gently heat the fruit, sugar and the water in a large heavy pan, shaking the pan occasionally, until the juices begin to run.

3 Reserve about 45ml/3 tbsp fruit juice, then spoon the fruit and remaining juice into the prepared bowl, taking care not to dislodge the bread lining.

4 Cut the remaining bread to fit entirely over the fruit. Stand the bowl on a plate and cover with a saucer or small plate that will just fit inside the top of the bowl. Place a heavy weight on top of the plate. Chill the pudding and the reserved fruit juice overnight in the refrigerator.

5 Run a knife carefully around the inside of the bowl rim, then invert the pudding on to a cold serving plate. Pour over the reserved juice, making sure that all the bread is completely covered, and serve.

Cook's Tips
• Use a good mix of summer fruits for this pudding – red- and blackcurrants, raspberries, strawberries and loganberries.
• Summer pudding freezes well so make an extra one to enjoy during the winter.

Chocolate Torte Energy 347kcal/1444kJ; Protein 3.7g; Carbohydrate 26.5g, of which sugars 25.9g; Fat 25.2g, of which saturates 15.3g; Cholesterol 89mg; Calcium 50mg; Fibre 1.2g; Sodium 138mg.
Summer Pudding Energy 211kcal/893kJ; Protein 6.2g; Carbohydrate 46.5g, of which sugars 21.3g; Fat 1.2g, of which saturates 0g; Cholesterol 0mg; Calcium 96mg; Fibre 3g; Sodium 293mg.

Gazpacho Juice

This is a light version of the classic Spanish soup, made without the usual bread, but making the most of the summer supply of tomatoes. It is the perfect refreshment after a day spent in the sunshine,

Serves 4–5
½ fresh red chilli
800g/1¾lb tomatoes, skinned

½ cucumber, roughly sliced
1 red (bell) pepper, seeded and
    cut into chunks
1 celery stick, chopped
1 spring onion (scallion),
    roughly chopped
a small handful of fresh coriander
    (cilantro), stalks included, plus
    extra to decorate
juice of 1 lime
salt
ice cubes

1 Using a sharp knife, seed the chilli. Add to a blender or food processor with the tomatoes, cucumber, red pepper, celery, spring onion and coriander.

2 Blend the mixture well until smooth, scraping the vegetable mixture down from the side of the bowl, if necessary, and blending again.

3 Add the lime juice and a little salt and blend. Pour into glasses or small bowls. Add ice cubes and a few coriander leaves and serve immediately.

Variation
If fresh chillies aren't available, soak 2 dried chillies in a little warm water for 20–30 minutes until they are rehydrated. Chop them and add to the juice as with the fresh variety above.

Cook's Tip
Ensure that you do not touch your eyes after chopping the fresh chilli. The oil from the chilli will aggravate your eyes. Make sure that you wash your hands in plenty of soapy water after preparing the chilli.

Red Defender

Boost your body's defences with this delicious blend of red fruits. Watermelon and strawberries are a good source of vitamin C and the black watermelon seeds, like all other seeds, are rich in essential nutrients. If you really don't like the idea of blending the seeds, remove them first.

Serves 2
200g/7oz/1¾ cups strawberries
small bunch red grapes,
    about 90g/3½oz
1 small wedge of watermelon

1 Hull the strawberries. Cut any berries in half if they are particularly large.

2 Pull the red grapes from their stalks. Cut away the skin from the watermelon using a knife or a vegetable peeler and chop into a few pieces.

3 Put the watermelon in a blender or food processor and blend until the seeds are broken up.

4 Add the strawberries and grapes and blend the mixture until completely smooth, scraping the mixture down from the side of the bowl, if necessary. Serve in tall glasses.

Variations
• Try this drink with other red summer fruits such as raspberries or redcurrants.
• Use green grapes, if you prefer, although the colour of the drink won't be quite as dramatic.

Cook's Tip
Decorate this juice with chunks of watermelon or strawberry halves, if you like.

Gazpacho Juice Energy 43kcal/183kJ; Protein 1.8g; Carbohydrate 7.9g, of which sugars 7.8g; Fat 0.7g, of which saturates 0.2g; Cholesterol 0mg; Calcium 24mg; Fibre 2.5g; Sodium 21mg.
Red Defender Energy 85kcal/362kJ; Protein 1.5g; Carbohydrate 20.1g, of which sugars 20.1g; Fat 0.5g, of which saturates 0.1g; Cholesterol 0mg; Calcium 29mg; Fibre 1.5g; Sodium 9mg.

Sparkling Peach Melba

Serve this delightfully fresh and fruity drink during the summer months when raspberries and peaches are at their sweetest and best. Traditional cream soda gives this drink a really smooth flavour and a lovely fizz, while the optional shot of Drambuie or brandy gives it a definite kick. Serve with long spoons for scooping up any fruit left in the glasses.

Serves 2
300g/11oz/scant 2 cups
raspberries
2 large ripe peaches
30ml/2 tbsp Drambuie or
brandy (optional)
15ml/1 tbsp icing
(confectioners') sugar
cream soda, to serve

1 Pack a few raspberries into six tiny shot glasses, or into six sections of an ice cube tray, and pour over water to cover. Freeze for several hours.

2 Using a small, sharp knife, halve and stone (pit) the peaches and cut one half into thin slices. Reserve 115g/4oz/⅔ cup of the raspberries and divide the rest, along with the peach slices, between two tall stemmed glasses. Drizzle with the Drambuie or brandy, if using.

3 Push the reserved raspberries and the remaining peach flesh through the juicer. Stir the icing sugar into the juice and pour the juice over the fruits.

4 Turn the raspberry-filled ice cubes out of the shot glasses or ice cube tray and add three to each glass. Top up with cream soda and serve immediately.

> **Cook's Tip**
> *If using shot glasses, dip these into a bowl of warm water for a few seconds to loosen the blocks of frozen raspberries. If using ice cube trays, turn these upside down and hold under warm running water for a few seconds. The ice cubes should then pop out easily.*

Purple Haze

Thick, dark blueberry purée swirled into pale and creamy vanilla-flavoured buttermilk looks stunning and tastes simply divine. Despite its creaminess, the buttermilk gives this sumptuous smoothie a delicious sharp tang. If you do not like buttermilk or cannot find it in your local supermarket, you could use a mixture of half natural yogurt and half milk instead.

Serves 2
250g/9oz/2¼ cups blueberries
50g/2oz/¼ cup caster
  (superfine) sugar
15ml/1 tbsp lemon juice
300ml/½ pint/1¼ cups
  buttermilk
5ml/1 tsp vanilla extract
150ml/¼ pint/⅔ cup full cream
  (whole) milk

1 Push the blueberries through a juicer and stir in 15ml/1 tbsp of the sugar and the lemon juice.

2 Stir the blueberry mixture well and divide it between two tall glasses.

3 Put the buttermilk, vanilla extract, milk and remaining sugar in a blender or food processor and blend until really frothy. (Alternatively, use a hand-held electric blender and blend until the mixture froths up.)

4 Pour the buttermilk mixture over the blueberry juice so the mixtures swirl together naturally – there is no need to stir them together as it tastes and looks better if they remain separate to a certain degree. Serve immediately.

> **Cook's Tip**
> *The deep violet blueberry juice in this drink makes a fantastic contrast in both colour and flavour to the buttermilk. If you cannot get hold of blueberries, other slightly tart summer fruits such as raspberries or blackberries would also work in this creamy combination.*

Purple Haze Energy 274kcal/1157kJ; Protein 9.1g; Carbohydrate 54.2g, of which sugars 49.2g; Fat 3.9g, of which saturates 2.4g; Cholesterol 13mg; Calcium 283mg; Fibre 2.5g; Sodium 99mg.
Sparkling Peach Melba Energy 100kcal/432kJ; Protein 3.2g; Carbohydrate 22.4g, of which sugars 22.4g; Fat 0.6g, of which saturates 0.2g; Cholesterol 0mg; Calcium 49mg; Fibre 5.3g; Sodium 6mg.

Sweet Potato and Parsnip Soup

The sweetness of two of the most popular root vegetables – which are used in both the main part of the dish and the garnish – comes through beautifully in this delicious soup. It is the ideal way to enjoy these typically autumn vegetables.

Serves 6
15ml/1 tbsp sunflower oil
1 large leek, sliced
2 celery sticks, chopped
450g/1 1b sweet potatoes, diced
225g/8oz parsnips, diced
900ml/1½ pints/3¾ cups
    vegetable stock
salt and ground black pepper

For the garnish
15ml/1 tbsp chopped
    fresh parsley
roasted strips of sweet potatoes
    and parsnips

1 Heat the oil in a large pan and add the leek, celery, sweet potatoes and parsnips. Cook gently for about 5 minutes, stirring to prevent them browning or sticking to the pan.

2 Stir in the vegetable stock and bring to the boil, then cover and simmer gently for about 25 minutes, or until the vegetables are tender, stirring occasionally. Season to taste with salt and ground black pepper. Remove the pan from the heat and allow the soup to cool slightly.

3 Purée the soup in a food processor or blender until smooth, then return the soup to the pan and reheat gently.

4 Ladle the soup into warmed soup bowls to serve and sprinkle over the chopped parsley and roasted strips of sweet potatoes and parsnips.

Cook's Tip
Making and freezing soup is a practical way of preserving a glut of root vegetables that are unlikely to keep well. Not only can excess raw vegetables be used this way, but leftover boiled, mashed or roasted root vegetables can all be added to soup, puréed, cooled or frozen.

Mixed Mushroom Soup

Mushrooms are one of the great joys of the autumn kitchen and this intensely flavoured soup is truly delicious. Serve little boiled potatoes on the side, to cut up and add as desired. The tart flavours of pickled cucumber, capers and lemon add extra bite to this rich mushroom medley.

25ml/1½ tbsp tomato
    purée (paste)
1 pickled cucumber, or
    dill pickle, chopped
1 bay leaf
15ml/1 tbsp capers in
    brine, drained
pinch of salt
6 peppercorns, crushed
675g/1½lb small potatoes
a little butter

Serves 4
2 onions, chopped
1.2 litres/2 pints/5 cups
    vegetable stock
450g/1lb mixed mushrooms, sliced

For the garnish
lemon rind curls
green olives
spring onions (scallions)
sprigs of flat leaf parsley

1 Put the onions in a large pan with 50ml/2fl oz/¼ cup of the stock. Cook, stirring occasionally, until the liquid has evaporated. Add the remaining vegetable stock with the sliced mushrooms. Bring to the boil, reduce the heat and cover the pan. Then simmer gently for 30 minutes.

2 In a small bowl, blend the tomato purée to a smooth, thin paste with about 30ml/2 tbsp of stock from the soup. Then stir the tomato mixture into the soup.

3 Add the pickled cucumber, bay leaf, capers, salt and peppercorns. Simmer the soup gently for another 10 minutes.

4 Meanwhile, place the potatoes in a pan and add water to cover. Bring to the boil, reduce the heat slightly and cook for about 10 minutes or until tender. Drain, place in a serving bowl and top with a little butter.

5 Ladle the soup into bowls. Sprinkle lemon rind curls, a few olives, sliced spring onions and a sprig of flat leaf parsley over each portion. Serve with the potatoes on the side.

Sweet Potato Soup Energy 113kcal/479kJ; Protein 2.1g; Carbohydrate 21.6g, of which sugars 7.2g; Fat 2.6g, of which saturates 0.4g; Cholesterol 0mg; Calcium 45mg; Fibre 4.3g; Sodium 40mg.
Mixed Mushroom Soup Energy 54kcal/224kJ; Protein 3.4g; Carbohydrate 8.9g, of which sugars 6.4g; Fat 0.8g, of which saturates 0.1g; Cholesterol 0mg; Calcium 33mg; Fibre 2.8g; Sodium 18mg.

Curried Pumpkin and Leek Soup

Ginger and cumin give this pumpkin soup a terrifically warm and spicy flavour. It makes a hearty, full-flavoured meal for a cold autumn night.

Serves 4
900g/2lb pumpkin, peeled and
  seeds removed
30ml/2 tbsp extra virgin olive oil
2 leeks, sliced
1 garlic clove, crushed
5ml/1 tsp ground ginger
5ml/1 tsp ground cumin
900ml/1½ pints/3¾ cups
  chicken stock
salt and ground black pepper
60ml/4 tbsp Greek (US strained
  plain) yogurt, to serve

1 Cut the pumpkin flesh into even chunks. Heat the oil in a large pan and add the leeks and garlic. Cover and cook gently, stirring occasionally, for about 15 minutes, until the vegetables are softened.

2 Add the ground ginger and cumin and cook, stirring, for a further 1 minute. Add the pumpkin chunks and the chicken stock and season with salt and pepper. Bring the mixture to the boil, reduce the heat and cover the pan. Then simmer for 30 minutes, or until the pumpkin is tender.

3 Process the soup, in batches if necessary, in a food processor or blender until smooth. Then return it to the rinsed-out pan.

4 Reheat the soup gently, and ladle out into four warmed individual bowls. Add a spoonful of Greek yogurt on the top of each and swirl it through the top layer of soup. Season with more ground black pepper, if you wish.

Variations
• Use marrow (large zucchini) instead of pumpkin and replace half the stock with coconut milk.
• For a slightly spicy twist, add a seeded and chopped fresh green chilli to the yogurt before swirling it into the soup.
• Use double the ginger and omit the cumin.

Pumpkin and Coconut Soup

This simple, yet punchy, autumn soup is rich with coconut balanced by an intriguing hint of sugar and spice. Just firm, but still fluffy, white rice provides an unusual garnish, but it is the perfect contrast for the silken texture of this soup. Following the amount given here, you should have just enough left over to serve as an accompaniment.

Serves 4
about 1.1kg/2lb 7oz pumpkin
750ml/1¼ pints/3 cups
  vegetable stock
750ml/1¼ pints/3 cups
  coconut milk
10–15ml/2–3 tsp sugar
115g/4oz/1 cup white rice
salt and ground black pepper
5ml/1 tsp ground cinnamon,
  to garnish

1 Remove any seeds or strands of fibre from the pumpkin, cut off the peel and chop the flesh. Put the prepared pumpkin in a pan and add the stock, coconut milk, sugar and seasoning.

2 Bring the soup to the boil, reduce the heat and cover. Simmer for about 20 minutes, until the pumpkin is tender. Purée the soup in a food processor or blender. Return it to the rinsed-out pan.

3 Place the rice in a pan and rinse it in several changes of cold water. Then drain in a sieve (strainer) and return it to the pan. Add plenty of fresh cold water to cover and bring to the boil. Stir once, reduce the heat and simmer for 15 minutes, until the grains are tender. Drain in a sieve (strainer).

4 Reheat the soup and taste it for seasoning, then ladle into bowls. Spoon a little rice into each portion and dust with cinnamon. Serve immediately, offering more rice at the table.

Variation
Use butternut squash in place of pumpkin, and brown rice in place of white rice, if you prefer. Both the butternut squash and the pumpkin are at their best in the autumn months.

Curried Pumpkin Soup Energy 98kcal/409kJ; Protein 3g; Carbohydrate 7.5g, of which sugars 5.8g; Fat 6.4g, of which saturates 1.1g; Cholesterol 0mg; Calcium 86mg; Fibre 4.2g; Sodium 2mg.
Pumpkin Soup Energy 148kcal/627kJ; Protein 8.8g; Carbohydrate 20.7g, of which sugars 13.5g; Fat 4g, of which saturates 2.3g; Cholesterol 11mg; Calcium 308mg; Fibre 2.8g; Sodium 81mg.

Marinated Mussels

Large, ultra-fresh mussels are one of the most eagerly awaited treats of autumn each year. Here they are served raw on the half shell in a flavoursome vinaigrette.

Serves 4–6
24 large live mussels, scrubbed and bearded
7.5ml/1½ tsp red wine vinegar or lemon juice
30ml/2 tbsp vegetable or olive oil
1 shallot, finely chopped
1 spring onion (scallion), finely chopped
1 medium ripe but firm tomato, finely chopped
salt and ground white pepper
30ml/2 tbsp freshly chopped parsley and 4–6 lemon wedges, to garnish
crusty bread, to serve

1 Discard any mussels that are not tightly closed, or which do not snap shut when tapped. Holding a mussel firmly between the thumb and index finger of one hand, carefully lever it open from the side with a sharp, short-bladed knife.

2 Insert the knife blade in the cavity and cut the muscle to which the mussel meat is attached. Work the knife blade around to free the mussel. Put it in a non-reactive bowl. Repeat the process with the remaining mussels. Wash and dry the mussel shells and save them.

3 In a separate bowl, whisk the vinegar or lemon juice with the oil. Season, then drizzle over the mussels. Fold in the shallot, spring onion and tomato. Cover and marinate in the refrigerator for at least 1 hour.

4 To serve, arrange half the mussel shells on a large platter and place a marinated mussel on each. Garnish with parsley and lemon wedges and serve with crusty bread.

Cook's Tips
• *Mussels for serving raw must be bought from a reputable fishmonger so they are guaranteed to be fresh.*
• *Marinated mussels can be kept in the refrigerator for 4 days.*

Garlic with Goat's Cheese Pâté

The combination of sweet roasted garlic and goat's cheese is a classic one. The pâté is flavoured with herbs and walnuts, which are hitting their peak in autumn.

Serves 4
4 large garlic bulbs
4 fresh rosemary sprigs
8 fresh thyme sprigs
60ml/4 tbsp olive oil
sea salt and ground black pepper
thyme sprigs, to garnish
4–8 slices sourdough bread and walnuts, to serve

For the pâté
200g/7oz/scant 1 cup soft goat's cheese
5ml/1 tsp finely chopped fresh thyme
15ml/1 tbsp chopped fresh parsley
50g/2oz/⅓ cup walnuts, chopped
15ml/1 tbsp walnut oil (optional)
fresh thyme, to garnish

1 Preheat the oven to 180°C/350°F/Gas 4. Strip the papery skin from the garlic bulbs. Place them in an ovenproof dish large enough to hold them snugly. Tuck in the fresh rosemary sprigs and fresh thyme sprigs, drizzle the olive oil over and season with a little sea salt and plenty of ground black pepper.

2 Cover the garlic tightly with foil and bake in the oven for 50–60 minutes, opening the parcel and basting once halfway through the cooking time. Set aside and leave to cool.

3 Preheat the grill (broiler). To make the pâté, cream the cheese with the thyme, parsley and chopped walnuts. Beat in 15ml/1 tbsp of the cooking oil from the garlic and season to taste with plenty of ground black pepper. Transfer the pâté to a serving bowl and chill until ready to serve.

4 Brush the sourdough bread slices on one side with the remaining cooking oil from the garlic bulbs, then grill (broil) until lightly toasted.

5 Divide the pâté among four plates. Drizzle the walnut oil, if using, over the goat's cheese pâté and grind some pepper over it. Place some garlic on each plate and serve with the pâté and some toasted bread. Garnish the pâté with a little fresh thyme and serve a few freshly shelled walnuts with each portion.

Goat's Cheese Pâté Energy 371kcal/1534kJ; Protein 14.5g; Carbohydrate 5.1g, of which sugars 1.3g; Fat 32.7g, of which saturates 11.3g; Cholesterol 47mg; Calcium 91mg; Fibre 1.7g; Sodium 304mg.
Marinated Mussels Energy 59kcal/246kJ; Protein 3.5g; Carbohydrate 1.8g, of which sugars 1.1g; Fat 4.3g, of which saturates 0.6g; Cholesterol 11mg; Calcium 14mg; Fibre 0.4g; Sodium 81mg.

Shelled Mussels with Garlic and Herbs

These mussels are served without their shells, in a delicious paprika-flavoured sauce. Eat them with cocktail sticks.

Serves 4
900g/2lb fresh mussels
1 lemon slice

90ml/6 tbsp olive oil
2 shallots, finely chopped
1 garlic clove, finely chopped
15ml/1 tbsp chopped
   fresh parsley
2.5ml/$\frac{1}{2}$ tsp sweet paprika
1.5ml/$\frac{1}{4}$ tsp dried chilli flakes

1 Scrub the mussels, discarding any damaged ones that do not close when tapped sharply with a knife. Place the mussels in a large pan, with about 250ml/8fl oz/1 cup water and the slice of lemon.

2 Bring the mixture to the boil and cook the mussels for about 3–4 minutes, removing the mussels as they open. Discard any that remain closed. Take the mussels out of the shells and drain on kitchen paper.

3 Heat the oil in a sauté pan, add the mussels and cook, stirring, for 1 minute. Remove from the pan.

4 Add the shallots and garlic and cook, covered, over low heat for about 5 minutes or until soft. Remove from the heat and stir in the parsley, paprika and chilli.

5 Return to the heat and stir in the mussels. Cook briefly. Remove from the heat and cover for a minute or two, to let the flavours mingle, before serving.

> **Cook's Tip**
> *If you prefer a little more heat in your food, then you can simply add a little more dried chilli flakes and paprika to the shallots and garlic in step 4.*

Deep-fried Layered Shiitake and Scallop

A wok does double duty for making these delicate mushroom and seafood treats, first for steaming and then for deep-frying.

Serves 4
4 scallops
8 large fresh shiitake mushrooms

225g/8oz long yam, unpeeled
20ml/4 tsp miso
50g/2oz/1 cup fresh breadcrumbs
cornflour (cornstarch), for dusting
2 eggs, beaten
vegetable oil, for deep-frying
salt
4 lemon wedges, to serve

1 Slice the scallops in two horizontally, then sprinkle with salt. Remove the stalks from the shiitake mushrooms and discard them. Cut shallow slits on the top of the shiitake to form a 'hash' symbol. Sprinkle with a little salt.

2 Heat a steamer and steam the long yam for 10–15 minutes, or until soft. Test with a skewer. Leave to cool, then remove the skin. Mash the flesh in a bowl, add the miso and mix well. Take the breadcrumbs into your hands and break them down finely. Mix half into the mashed long yam, keeping the rest on a small plate.

3 Fill the underneath of the shiitake caps with a scoop of mashed long yam. Smooth down with the flat edge of a knife and dust the mash with cornflour. Add a little mash to a slice of scallop and place on top.

4 Spread another 5ml/1 tsp mashed long yam on to the scallop and shape to completely cover. Make sure all the ingredients are clinging together. Repeat to make eight little mounds.

5 Place the beaten eggs in a shallow container. Dust the shiitake and scallop mounds with cornflour, then dip into the egg. Handle with care as the mash and scallop are quite soft. Coat well with the remaining breadcrumbs and deep-fry in hot oil until golden. Drain well on kitchen paper. Serve hot on individual plates with a wedge of lemon.

Mussels with Herbs Energy 214kcal/888kJ; Protein 12g; Carbohydrate 1.3g, of which sugars 0.9g; Fat 17.9g, of which saturates 2.6g; Cholesterol 27mg; Calcium 145mg; Fibre 0.4g; Sodium 144mg.
Shiitake and Scallop Energy 812kcal/3396kJ; Protein 45.8g; Carbohydrate 54g, of which sugars 12.6g; Fat 47.8g, of which saturates 7.5g; Cholesterol 428mg; Calcium 279mg; Fibre 7g; Sodium 741mg.

Warm Halloumi and Fennel Salad

The firm texture of halloumi cheese makes it perfect for the barbecue, as it keeps its shape very well. Combined with the delicate flavour of seasonal fennel, it makes a lovely chargrilled salad.

2 fennel bulbs, trimmed
  and thinly sliced
30ml/2 tbsp roughly chopped
  fresh oregano
45ml/3 tbsp lemon-infused
  olive oil
salt and ground black pepper

Serves 4
200g/7oz halloumi cheese,
  thickly sliced

1 Place the halloumi, fennel and oregano in a mixing bowl and drizzle over the lemon-infused oil. Season with salt and black pepper to taste. Mix together the ingredients until they are thoroughly combined.

2 Cover the bowl with a piece of clear film (plastic wrap) and chill in the refrigerator for about 2 hours to allow all the flavours to develop.

3 Heat a griddle pan on the stove until very hot, or light a barbecue and wait until there is a coating of ash on the coals.

4 Place the halloumi and fennel on a griddle pan or over the barbecue, reserving the marinade, and cook for about 3 minutes on each side, until charred.

5 Divide the halloumi and fennel among four serving plates and drizzle over the reserved marinade. Serve immediately.

Cook's Tips
• Fennel is often on its way out of season as autumn comes to an end and winter begins, so make the most of this tasty, underrated vegetable.
• Halloumi is a fairly salty cheese, so be very careful when adding extra salt.

Grilled Fennel Salad

Fennel has many fans, but is often used only in its raw state or lightly braised, making this griddle recipe a delightful discovery for ways to treat this delicious autumn vegetable.

30ml/2 tbsp olive oil
15ml/1 tbsp cider or white
  wine vinegar
45ml/3 tbsp extra virgin olive oil
24 small Niçoise olives
2 long sprigs of fresh savory,
  leaves removed
salt and ground black pepper

Serves 6
3 sweet baby orange
  (bell) peppers
5 fennel bulbs with green tops,
  about 900g/2lb total weight

1 Heat a griddle until a few drops of water sprinkled on to the surface evaporate instantly. Grill (broil) the baby peppers, turning them every few minutes until charred all over. Remove the pan from the heat, place the peppers in a bowl and cover with clear film (plastic wrap).

2 Remove the green fronds from the fennel and reserve. Slice the fennel lengthways into five roughly equal pieces. If the root looks a little tough, cut it out. Place the fennel pieces in a flat dish, coat with the olive oil and season with salt and pepper. Rub off the charred skin from the grilled peppers, remove the seeds and cut the flesh into small dice.

3 Re-heat the griddle and test the temperature again, then lower the heat slightly and grill (broil) the fennel slices in batches for about 8–10 minutes, turning frequently, until they are branded with golden grill marks. Monitor the heat so they cook through without over charring. As each batch cooks, transfer it to a flat serving dish.

4 Whisk the vinegar and extra virgin olive oil together in a small bowl, then pour over the fennel. Gently fold in the diced baby orange peppers and the Niçoise olives. Roughly tear the savory leaves and fennel fronds and sprinkle over the salad. Serve warm.

Warm Halloumi Salad Energy 215kcal/889kJ; Protein 10.2g; Carbohydrate 1.8g, of which sugars 1.7g; Fat 18.6g, of which saturates 8.1g; Cholesterol 29mg; Calcium 205mg; Fibre 2.4g; Sodium 209mg.
Grilled Fennel Salad Energy 139kcal/574kJ; Protein 2.4g; Carbohydrate 8.7g, of which sugars 8.3g; Fat 10.8g, of which saturates 1.6g; Cholesterol 0mg; Calcium 49mg; Fibre 5.3g; Sodium 208mg.

Marinated Button Mushrooms with Sherry

This Spanish dish makes a refreshing alternative to the ever-popular mushrooms fried in garlic.

Serves 4
30ml/2 tbsp extra virgin olive oil
1 small onion, very finely chopped
1 garlic clove, finely chopped
15ml/1 tbsp tomato
   purée (paste)
50ml/2fl oz/¼ cup
   amontillado sherry
50ml/2fl oz/¼ cup water
2 cloves
225g/8oz/3 cups button (white)
   mushrooms, trimmed
salt and ground black pepper
chopped fresh parsley,
   to garnish

1 Heat the oil in a pan. Add the onion and garlic and cook until soft. Stir in the tomato purée, sherry, water and the cloves and season with salt and black pepper.

2 Bring the mixture to the boil, cover the pan and simmer gently for about 45 minutes, adding more water if the mixture becomes too dry.

3 Add the mushrooms to the pan, then cover and allow to simmer for about 5 minutes. Remove from the heat and allow to cool, still covered.

4 Chill the mushrooms in the refrigerator overnight so that they take on the flavours. Serve the salad cold, sprinkled with the chopped parsley.

Cook's Tip
One of the joys of autumn is the plentiful supply of mushrooms. You can use free wild mushrooms for this dish if you are lucky enough to live near a woodland where you can go and pick your own. When picking wild mushrooms, remember to carry them in a basket so that their spores can drop on to the ground as you wander around the area.

Fragrant Mushrooms in Lettuce Leaves

This quick and easy autumn salad is a perfect way to enjoy the abundance of mushrooms at this time of year. Served on leaves, they make great finger food.

Serves 2
30ml/2 tbsp vegetable oil
2 garlic cloves, finely chopped
2 baby cos or romaine lettuces,
   or 2 Little Gem (Bibb) lettuces
1 lemon grass stalk, finely chopped
2 kaffir lime leaves, rolled in
   cylinders and thinly sliced
200g/7oz/3 cups oyster or
   chestnut mushrooms, sliced
1 small fresh red chilli, seeded
   and finely chopped
juice of ½ lemon
30ml/2 tbsp light soy sauce
5ml/1 tsp palm sugar (jaggery) or
   light muscovado (brown) sugar
1 small bunch fresh mint, leaves
   removed from the stalks

1 Heat the oil in a wok or frying pan. Add the garlic and cook over medium heat, stirring occasionally, until golden. Do not let it burn or it will taste bitter.

2 Meanwhile, divide up the lettuces into separate, individual leaves and set aside.

3 Increase the heat under the wok or pan and add the lemon grass, lime leaves and mushrooms. Stir-fry for about 2 minutes.

4 Add the chilli, lemon juice, soy sauce and sugar to the wok or pan. Toss the mixture over the heat to combine the ingredients together, then stir-fry for a further 2 minutes.

5 Arrange the lettuce leaves on a large plate. Spoon a little mushroom mixture on to each leaf, top with a mint leaf and serve immediately.

Cook's Tip
If you can't find kaffir leaves, you can use freshly grated lime rind instead.

Marinated Mushrooms Energy 80kcal/329kJ; Protein 1.4g; Carbohydrate 2.1g, of which sugars 1.7g; Fat 5.8g, of which saturates 0.9g; Cholesterol 0mg; Calcium 9mg; Fibre 0.9g; Sodium 14mg.
Fragrant Mushrooms Energy 162kcal/672kJ; Protein 4.6g; Carbohydrate 7.9g, of which sugars 6.3g; Fat 12.7g, of which saturates 1.6g; Cholesterol 0mg; Calcium 117mg; Fibre 2.9g; Sodium 549mg.

Sweet Pumpkin and Peanut Curry

Rich, sweet, spicy and fragrant, the flavours of this Thai-style curry really come together during the long simmering in the slow cooker. Serve with rice or noodles for a supper dish on a cold autumn night.

Serves 4
30ml/2 tbsp vegetable oil
4 garlic cloves, crushed
4 shallots, finely chopped
30ml/2 tbsp yellow curry paste
2 kaffir lime leaves, torn
15ml/1 tbsp chopped
   fresh galangal

450g/1lb pumpkin, peeled, seeded
   and diced
225g/8oz sweet potatoes, diced
400ml/14fl oz/1²⁄₃ cups
   near-boiling vegetable stock
300ml/¹⁄₂ pint/1¹⁄₄ cups
   coconut milk
90g/3¹⁄₂oz/1¹⁄₂ cups chestnut
   mushrooms, sliced
15ml/1 tbsp soy sauce
90g/3¹⁄₂oz/scant 1 cup peanuts,
   roasted and chopped
50g/2oz/¹⁄₃ cup pumpkin seeds,
   toasted, and fresh green chilli
   flowers, to garnish

1 Heat the oil in a frying pan. Add the garlic and shallots and cook over medium heat, stirring occasionally, for 10 minutes, until softened and beginning to turn golden.

2 Add the yellow curry paste to the pan and stir-fry over medium heat for 30 seconds, until fragrant. Transfer the mixture to the ceramic cooking pot.

3 Add the lime leaves, galangal, pumpkin and sweet potatoes to the cooking pot. Pour the hot vegetable stock and about 150ml/¹⁄₄ pint/²⁄₃ cup of the coconut milk over the vegetables, and stir to combine. Cover with the lid and cook on the high setting for 1¹⁄₂ hours.

4 Stir the mushrooms and soy sauce into the curry, then add the chopped peanuts and pour in the remaining coconut milk. Cover and cook on high for a further 3 hours, or until the vegetables are very tender.

5 Spoon the curry into warmed serving bowls, garnish with the pumpkin seeds and chillies, and serve immediately.

Pumpkin with Spices

Roasted pumpkin has a wonderful, rich flavour redolent of autumn. Eat it straight from the skin, eat the skin too, or scoop out the cooked flesh, add a spoonful of a spicy tomato salsa and wrap it in a warm tortilla. It is also good for making flavoursome soups and tasty sauces.

Serves 6
1kg/2¹⁄₄lb pumpkin
50g/2oz/¹⁄₄ cup butter
10ml/2 tsp hot chilli sauce
2.5ml/¹⁄₂ tsp salt
2.5ml/¹⁄₂ tsp ground allspice
5ml/1 tsp ground cinnamon
chopped fresh herbs, to garnish
spicy tomato salsa and crème
   fraîche, to serve

1 Preheat the oven to 220°C/425°F/Gas 7. Cut the pumpkin into large pieces. Scoop out and discard the fibre and seeds, then put the pumpkin pieces in a roasting pan.

2 Melt the butter in a pan over low heat, or in a heatproof bowl in the microwave. Mix together the melted butter and chilli sauce and drizzle the mixture evenly over the pumpkin pieces in the roasting pan.

3 Put the salt in a small bowl and add the ground allspice and cinnamon. Mix together well and sprinkle the mixture over the pumpkin pieces.

4 Place the roasting pan in the oven and roast for 25 minutes, turning halfway through the cooking. The pumpkin flesh should yield when pressed gently, if it is ready.

5 Transfer the spiced pumpkin pieces to a warmed serving dish and serve. Offer the salsa and crème fraîche separately.

Cook's Tip
Green, grey or orange-skinned pumpkins all roast well and would work in this recipe. The orange-fleshed varieties are, however, the most vibrantly coloured and will look wonderful when used in this dish.

Pumpkin with Spices Energy 84kcal/347kJ; Protein 1.2g; Carbohydrate 3.7g, of which sugars 2.9g; Fat 7.2g, of which saturates 4.5g; Cholesterol 18mg; Calcium 50mg; Fibre 1.7g; Sodium 214mg.
Sweet Pumpkin Curry Energy 337kcal/1404kJ; Protein 10.3g; Carbohydrate 21.7g, of which sugars 10.8g; Fat 23.8g, of which saturates 4g; Cholesterol 0mg; Calcium 168mg; Fibre 5.1g; Sodium 554mg.

Pumpkin Gnocchi with Chanterelle Parsley Cream

Pumpkin adds a sweetness to these potato gnocchi, which are superb on their own or served with meat.

Serves 4

450g/1lb pumpkin, peeled, seeded and chopped
450g/1lb potatoes, boiled
2 egg yolks
200g/7oz/1¾ cups plain (all-purpose) flour, plus more if necessary
pinch of ground allspice
1.5ml/¼ tsp cinnamon
pinch of freshly grated nutmeg
finely grated rind of ½ orange
salt and ground black pepper

For the sauce
30ml/2 tbsp olive oil
1 shallot, finely chopped
175g/6oz fresh chanterelles, sliced, or 15g/½oz dried, soaked in warm water for 20 minutes, then drained
10ml/2 tsp almond butter
150ml/¼ pint/⅔ cup crème fraîche
75ml/5 tbsp chopped fresh parsley
50g/2oz/½ cup Parmesan cheese, freshly grated

1 Wrap the pumpkin in foil and bake at 180°C/350°F/Gas 4 for 30 minutes. Pass the pumpkin and cooked potatoes through a food mill into a bowl. Add the egg yolks, flour, spices, orange rind and seasoning and mix well to make a soft dough. If the mixture is too loose add a little flour to stiffen it.

2 To make the sauce, heat the oil in a pan and fry the shallot until soft. Add the chanterelles and cook briefly, then add the almond butter. Stir to melt and stir in the crème fraîche. Simmer briefly, add the parsley and season to taste. Keep hot.

3 Flour a work surface. Spoon the gnocchi dough into a piping (pastry) bag fitted with a 1cm/½in plain nozzle. Pipe on to the flour to make a 15cm/6in sausage. Roll in flour and cut crossways into 2.5cm/1in pieces. Repeat. Mark each piece lightly with a fork and drop into a pan of fast boiling salted water.

4 The gnocchi are done when they rise to the surface, after 3–4 minutes. Drain and turn into bowls. Spoon the sauce over, sprinkle with Parmesan, and serve immediately.

Spiced Couscous with Halloumi and Courgette Ribbons

Couscous forms the foundation of this dish and is topped with griddled, sliced courgettes and halloumi.

Serves 4

275g/10oz/1⅔ cups couscous
1 bay leaf
1 cinnamon stick
30ml/2 tbsp olive oil, plus extra for brushing
1 large red onion, chopped
2 garlic cloves, chopped
5ml/1 tsp mild chilli powder
5ml/1 tsp ground cumin
5ml/1 tsp ground coriander
5 cardamom pods, bruised
50g/2oz/¼ cup whole almonds, toasted
1 peach, stoned (pitted) and diced
25g/1oz/2 tbsp butter
3 courgettes (zucchini), sliced lengthways into ribbons
225g/8oz halloumi cheese, sliced
salt and ground black pepper
chopped fresh flat leaf parsley, to garnish

1 Place the couscous in a bowl and pour over 500ml/17fl oz/ generous 2 cups boiling water. Add the bay leaf and cinnamon stick and season with salt. Leave the couscous for 10 minutes until the water is absorbed, then fluff up the grains with a fork.

2 Meanwhile, heat the oil in a large heavy pan, add the onion and garlic and cook, stirring, for about 7 minutes until soft.

3 Stir in the chilli powder, cumin, coriander and cardamom pods, and cook for 3 minutes. Add the couscous, almonds, diced peach and butter, and heat through for 2 minutes.

4 Brush a griddle pan with oil and heat until very hot. Turn down the heat to medium, then place the courgettes on the griddle and cook for 5 minutes until tender and slightly charred. Turn the courgettes over, add the halloumi and continue cooking for 5 minutes, turning the halloumi halfway through.

5 Remove the cinnamon stick, bay leaf and cardamom pods from the couscous, then arrange it on a plate and season well. Top with the halloumi and courgettes. Sprinkle the parsley over the top and serve.

Pumpkin Gnocchi Energy 553kcal/2317kJ; Protein 15.6g; Carbohydrate 61.7g, of which sugars 5.9g; Fat 28.8g, of which saturates 14.7g; Cholesterol 156mg; Calcium 299mg; Fibre 4.5g; Sodium 166mg.
Spiced Couscous Energy 515kcal/2138kJ; Protein 19.9g; Carbohydrate 42.7g, of which sugars 6.1g; Fat 30.3g, of which saturates 12.5g; Cholesterol 46mg; Calcium 290mg; Fibre 2.9g; Sodium 264mg.

Mushroom Stroganoff

This creamy mixed mushroom sauce tastes great and is ideal for an autumn dinner party. Serve it with toasted buckwheat, brown rice or a mix of wild rices. Ribbon noodles also make a good accompaniment. Cook them in boiling water or stock then toss them in a little olive oil.

Serves 8
25g/1oz/2 tbsp butter
900g/2lb/8 cups mixed
   mushrooms, cut into
   bitesize pieces
350g/12oz/1¾ cups white long
   grain rice
350ml/12fl oz/1½ cups white
   wine sauce
250ml/8fl oz/1 cup sour cream
salt and ground black pepper
chopped chives, to garnish

1 Melt the butter in a large pan and cook the mushrooms over medium heat until they give up their liquid. Cook until they are tender and beginning to reabsorb the pan juices and brown.

2 Meanwhile, bring a large pan of lightly salted water to the boil. Add the rice, partially cover the pan and cook over medium heat for 13–15 minutes until the rice is just tender.

3 Add the wine sauce to the cooked mushrooms in the pan and bring to the boil, stirring. Stir in the sour cream and season to taste with salt and pepper.

4 Drain the rice well, spoon on to warm plates, top with the sauce and garnish with chives. Serve immediately.

Cook's Tip
Although you can make this with regular button (white) mushrooms, it is especially delicious with wild mushrooms such as ceps or oyster mushrooms. When wild fungi are plentiful, in the autumn, farmers' markets are a good source. You may even be able to find more unusual specimens such as chicken of the woods, chanterelles, cauliflower fungus, morels or wood blewits. If you pick wild mushrooms yourself, make sure you know exactly what you are doing – mistakes can be deadly.

Garlic Chive Rice with Mushrooms

A wide range of mushrooms is readily available in the autumn. They combine well with rice and garlic chives to make a tasty dish.

Serves 4
350g/12oz/generous 1¾ cups
   long grain rice, washed
60ml/4 tbsp groundnut (peanut) oil
1 small onion, finely chopped
2 green chillies, seeded and chopped
25g/1oz garlic chives, chopped
15g/½oz fresh coriander (cilantro)
600ml/1 pint/2½ cups vegetable
   or mushroom stock
2.5ml/½ tsp sea salt
250g/9oz mixed mushrooms,
   thickly sliced
50g/2oz cashew nuts, fried in
   15ml/1 tbsp olive oil until
   golden brown
ground black pepper

1 Drain the rice. Heat half the oil in a pan and cook the onion and chillies over low heat, stirring, for 10–12 minutes until soft.

2 Set half the chives aside. Cut the stalks off the coriander and set the leaves aside. Purée the remaining chives and the coriander stalks with the stock in a food processor or blender.

3 Add the rice to the onions and fry over low heat, stirring frequently, for 4–5 minutes. Pour in the stock mixture, then add the salt and some black pepper. Bring to the boil, stir well and reduce the heat to very low. Cover with a lid and cook for 15–20 minutes, or until the rice has absorbed all the liquid.

4 Remove the pan from the heat and lay a clean, folded dish towel over the pan, under the lid, and press on the lid to wedge it firmly in place. Leave the rice to stand for a further 10 minutes, allowing the towel to absorb the steam while the rice becomes completely tender.

5 Meanwhile, heat the remaining oil in a frying pan and cook the mushrooms for 5–6 minutes until tender and browned. Stir in the remaining garlic chives and cook for 1–2 minutes.

6 Stir the mushroom and chive mixture and coriander leaves into the rice. Adjust the seasoning, then transfer to a warmed serving dish, sprinkled with the fried cashew nuts.

Stroganoff Energy 556kcal/2316kJ; Protein 13.3g; Carbohydrate 80.4g, of which sugars 7.2g; Fat 21.7g, of which saturates 11.4g; Cholesterol 51mg; Calcium 96mg; Fibre 2.5g; Sodium 897mg.
Garlic Chive Rice Energy 504kcal/2100kJ; Protein 10.4g; Carbohydrate 73.8g, of which sugars 1.8g; Fat 18.2g, of which saturates 2.6g; Cholesterol 0mg; Calcium 41mg; Fibre 1.6g; Sodium 533mg.

Spicy Root Vegetable Gratin

Subtly spiced, this rich gratin is slowly baked in the oven and is substantial enough to serve on its own for lunch or supper. It is also perfect as a tasty side dish to accompany grilled meats.

Serves 4
2 large potatoes, total weight about 450g/1lb
2 sweet potatoes, total weight about 275g/10oz
175g/6oz celeriac

15ml/1 tbsp unsalted butter
5ml/1 tsp curry powder
5ml/1 tsp ground turmeric
2.5ml/½ tsp ground coriander
5ml/1 tsp mild chilli powder
3 shallots, chopped
150ml/¼ pint/⅔ cup single (light) cream
150ml/¼ pint/⅔ cup milk
salt and ground black pepper
chopped fresh flat leaf parsley, to garnish

1 Peel the potatoes, sweet potatoes and celeriac and cut into thin, even slices using a sharp knife or the slicing attachment on a food processor. Immediately place the vegetables in a bowl of cold water to prevent them from discolouring.

2 Preheat the oven to 180°C/350°F/Gas 4. Heat half the butter in a heavy pan, add the curry powder, ground turmeric and coriander and half the chilli powder. Cook for 2 minutes, then leave to cool slightly.

3 Drain the vegetables, then pat them dry with kitchen paper. Place in a bowl, add the spice mixture and the shallots, and mix well. Arrange the vegetables in a shallow baking dish, seasoning well with salt and pepper between the layers.

4 In a bowl, mix together the cream and milk until well blended. Pour the mixture over the vegetables in the dish, then sprinkle the remaining chilli powder on top.

5 Cover the dish with baking parchment and bake for about 45 minutes. Remove the baking parchment, dot the vegetables with the remaining butter and bake for a further 50 minutes, or until the top is golden brown. Serve the gratin garnished with chopped parsley.

Onions Stuffed with Goat's Cheese

Long, gentle cooking is the best way to get maximum flavour from onions, so the slow cooker is the natural choice for this delicious stuffed-onion dish.

Serves 4
2 large onions, unpeeled
30ml/2 tbsp olive oil (or use oil from the sun-dried tomatoes)
150g/5oz/⅔ cup firm goat's cheese, crumbled or cubed

50g/2oz/1 cup fresh white breadcrumbs
8 sun-dried tomatoes in olive oil, drained and chopped
1 garlic clove, finely chopped
2.5ml/½ tsp fresh thyme
30ml/2 tbsp chopped fresh parsley
1 small egg, beaten
45ml/3 tbsp pine nuts
150ml/¼ pint/⅔ cup near-boiling vegetable stock
salt and ground black pepper
chopped fresh parsley, to garnish

1 Bring a large pan of water to the boil. Add the whole onions in their skins and boil for 10 minutes.

2 Drain the onions and leave until cool enough to handle, then cut each onion in half horizontally and peel. Using a teaspoon, remove the centre of each onion, leaving a thick shell.

3 Very finely chop the flesh from one of the scooped-out onion halves and place in a bowl. Stir in 5ml/1 tsp of the olive oil or oil from the sun-dried tomatoes, then add the goat's cheese, breadcrumbs, sun-dried tomatoes, garlic, thyme, parsley, egg and pine nuts. Season with salt and pepper and mix well.

4 Divide the stuffing among the onions and cover each one with a piece of oiled foil. Brush the base of the ceramic cooking pot with 15ml/1 tbsp of oil, then pour in the stock. Put the onions in the base of the cooking pot, cover with the lid and cook on high for 4 hours, or until the onions are tender but still hold their shape.

5 Remove the onions from the slow cooker and transfer them to a grill (broiler) pan. Remove the foil and drizzle with the remaining oil. Brown the tops of the onions under the grill for 3–4 minutes, taking care not to burn the nuts. Serve immediately, garnished with parsley.

Spicy Gratin Energy 268kcal/1129kJ; Protein 5.8g; Carbohydrate 37.7g, of which sugars 9.8g; Fat 11.6g, of which saturates 7.1g; Cholesterol 31mg; Calcium 127mg; Fibre 3.6g; Sodium 117mg.
Onions Stuffed Energy 330kcal/1370kJ; Protein 13.8g; Carbohydrate 14.3g, of which sugars 11.3g; Fat 24.7g, of which saturates 8.4g; Cholesterol 83.7mg; Calcium 98mg; Fibre 1.9g; Sodium 349mg.

Steamed Mussels with Onions and Celery

One of the best ways of preparing this dish is to simply steam the mussels in their own juices with celery and onions. This allows the delectable flavour of the mussels to shine through.

Serves 4
4kg/9lb live mussels
40g/1½oz/3 tbsp
 butter, softened

2 onions, roughly chopped
3–4 celery sticks, roughly chopped
salt and ground white pepper
chopped fresh parsley, to garnish
fries or crusty bread and
 pickles or mayonnaise,
 to serve

1 Scrub the mussels until the shells are shiny black and smooth. Remove beards, if present. If any of the shells are cracked or broken, discard them, along with any mussels that are open and that do not snap shut if tapped.

2 Melt the butter in a large heavy pan over medium heat. Add the onions and sauté for 5 minutes until softened and glazed. Add the celery and sauté for 5 minutes more. Add the mussels and season generously with salt and pepper.

3 Cover the pan and cook over high heat for 3–4 minutes or until the mussels open, shaking the pan occasionally to distribute the steam. Discard any mussels that do not open. Taste the liquid in the pan and adjust the seasoning if necessary, then spoon the mussels and the liquid into bowls or pots.

4 Sprinkle with parsley and serve with fries or crusty bread. Offer pickles, mayonnaise or mustard vinaigrette on the side.

> **Variation**
> *A splash of white wine, poured over the mussels before cooking, improves the dish, and a little hot mustard can also be added.*

Mussels in a Cider and Cream Broth

Mussels are delicious in the autumn when steamed and lifted out of their shells, and quickly fried with bacon. Here they are cooked with a broth of cider, garlic and cream. Serve the mussels in large shallow bowls with a chunk of bread to mop up the juices. Don't forget to provide finger bowls for cleaning sticky fingers.

Serves 4
1.8kg/4lb mussels in their shells
40g/1½oz/3 tbsp butter
1 leek, washed and finely chopped
1 garlic clove, finely chopped
150ml/¼ pint/⅔ cup dry
 (hard) cider
30–45ml/2–3 tbsp double
 (heavy) cream
a handful of fresh
 parsley, chopped
ground black pepper

1 Scrub the mussels and scrape off any barnacles. Discard those with broken shells or that refuse to close when given a sharp tap with a knife. Pull off the hairy beards from the mussels with a sharp tug.

2 Melt the butter in a very large pan and add the leek and garlic. Cook over medium heat for about 5 minutes, stirring frequently, until very soft but not browned. Season with pepper.

3 Add the cider and immediately tip in the mussels. Cover with a lid and cook quickly, shaking the pan occasionally, until the mussels have just opened (take care not to overcook and toughen them).

4 Remove the lid, add the cream and parsley and bubble gently for a minute or two. Serve immediately in shallow bowls.

> **Cook's Tips**
> *Eat mussels the fun way! Use an empty shell as pincers to pick out the mussels from the other shells. Don't try to eat any whose shells have not opened during cooking or you risk food poisoning. Provide an empty bowl for the mussel shells.*

Mussels in Cider Energy 261kcal/1092kJ; Protein 21.1g; Carbohydrate 6.5g, of which sugars 2.1g; Fat 15.6g, of which saturates 8.2g; Cholesterol 104mg; Calcium 82mg; Fibre 1g; Sodium 498mg.
Steamed Mussels Energy 393kcal/1658kJ; Protein 46.5g; Carbohydrate 17.3g, of which sugars 6g; Fat 15.5g, of which saturates 6.2g; Cholesterol 181mg; Calcium 183mg; Fibre 1.9g; Sodium 1048mg.

Mussel Risotto

The addition of freshly cooked mussels, aromatic coriander and a little cream to a packet of instant risotto can turn a simple meal into a decadent treat. Serve with a side salad for a splendid autumnal supper. Other types of cooked shellfish, such as clams or prawns, can be used instead of mussels.

Serves 3–4
900g/2lb fresh mussels
275g/10oz packet risotto
30ml/2 tbsp chopped fresh
   coriander (cilantro)
30ml/2 tbsp double
   (heavy) cream

1 Scrub the mussels, discarding any that do not close when sharply tapped. Place in a large pan. Add 120ml/4fl oz/½ cup water and seasoning, then bring to the boil. Cover the pan and cook the mussels, shaking the pan occasionally, for 4–5 minutes, until they have opened. Drain, reserving the liquid and discarding any that have not opened. Shell most of the mussels, reserving a few in their shells for garnish. Strain the mussel liquid.

2 Make up the packet risotto according to the instructions, using the cooking liquid from the mussels and making it up to the required volume with water.

3 When the risotto is about three-quarters cooked, add the mussels to the pan. Add the coriander and re-cover the pan without stirring in these ingredients.

4 Remove the risotto from the heat, stir in the cream, cover and leave to rest for a few minutes. Spoon into a warmed serving dish, garnish with the reserved mussels in their shells, and serve.

> **Cook's Tip**
> For a super-quick mussel risotto, use cooked mussels in their shells – the type sold vacuum packed ready to reheat. Just reheat them according to the packet instructions and add to the made risotto with the coriander and cream.

Clams and Mussels in Banana Leaves

Autumn is the perfect time for these tasty, pretty parcels. It is the ideal dish to make the most of the clams and mussels during the season.

Serves 6
15ml/1 tbsp olive oil
1 large onion, finely chopped
2 garlic cloves, crushed
1.5ml/¼ tsp saffron threads
60ml/4 tbsp Noilly Prat or other
   dry vermouth
30ml/2 tbsp water
30ml/2 tbsp chopped fresh flat
   leaf parsley
500g/1¼lb clams, scrubbed
900g/2lb cleaned mussels
6 banana leaves
salt and ground black pepper
raffia, for tying
bread sticks, for serving

1 Heat the oil in a pan and cook the onion and garlic with the saffron threads over low heat for 4 minutes. Add the vermouth and water, and simmer for 2 minutes. Stir in the parsley, with seasoning to taste. Transfer to a bowl and leave to cool.

2 Tap the clam and mussel shells and discard any that stay open. Stir them into the bowl containing the onion mixture. Trim the hard edge from each banana leaf and discard it. Cut the leaves in half lengthways. Soak in hot water for 10 minutes, then drain. Rinse, then pour over boiling water to soften.

3 Top a sheet of foil with a piece of banana leaf, placing it smooth-side up. Place another piece of leaf on top, at right angles, so that the leaves form a cross.

4 Pile one-sixth of the seafood mixture into the centre, then bring up the leaves and tie them into a money-bag shape, using lengths of raffia. Do the same with the foil, scrunching slightly to seal the top. Make the remaining parcels in the same way, then chill the parcels until needed.

5 Prepare the barbecue. Once the flames have died down, position a lightly oiled grill rack over the coals to heat. When the coals are medium-hot, or with a moderate coating of ash, cook the parcels for 15 minutes. Remove the outer layer of foil from each and put the parcels back on the grill rack for 1 minute. Transfer to plates and serve with bread sticks.

Mussel Risotto Energy 439kcal/1833kJ; Protein 17.2g; Carbohydrate 56.6g, of which sugars 1.4g; Fat 11.3g, of which saturates 3.5g; Cholesterol 37mg; Calcium 159mg; Fibre 0.2g; Sodium 146mg.
Clams and Mussels Energy 116kcal/488kJ; Protein 14g; Carbohydrate 6.2g, of which sugars 4g; Fat 3.1g, of which saturates 0.5g; Cholesterol 40mg; Calcium 131mg; Fibre 0.9g; Sodium 498mg.

Scallops with Fennel, Mascarpone and Bacon

This dish is a delicious combination of succulent seasonal scallops and crispy bacon, served on a bed of tender fennel and melting mascarpone. If you can't get large scallops (known as king scallops), buy the smaller queen scallops and serve a dozen per person. If you buy scallops in the shell, wash and keep the pretty fan-shaped shells to serve a range of fish dishes in.

Serves 2
2 small fennel bulbs
130g/4¹/₂oz/generous ¹/₂ cup
  mascarpone cheese
8 large scallops, shelled
75g/3oz thin smoked streaky
  (fatty) bacon rashers (strips)
salt and ground black pepper

1 Trim, halve and slice the fennel, reserving and chopping any feathery tops. Blanch in boiling water for 3 minutes. Drain.

2 Preheat the grill (broiler) to moderate. Place the fennel in a shallow flameproof dish and season with salt and pepper. Dot with the mascarpone and grill (broil) for about 5 minutes, until the cheese has melted and the fennel is lightly browned.

3 Meanwhile, pat the scallops dry on kitchen paper and season lightly. Cook the bacon in a large, heavy frying pan, until crisp and golden, turning once. Drain and keep warm. Fry the scallops in the pan for 1–2 minutes on each side, until cooked through.

4 Transfer the fennel to serving plates and crumble or snip the bacon into bitesize pieces over the top. Pile the scallops on the bacon and sprinkle with any reserved fennel tops.

Cook's Tip
Choose fresh rather than frozen scallops as the frozen ones tend to exude water on cooking. Have the pan very hot as scallops need only the briefest cooking at high heat – just until they turn opaque and brown on each side.

Scallops and Tiger Prawns

Serve this light, delicate dish for lunch or supper accompanied by aromatic steamed rice or fine rice noodles and stir-fried pak choi or broccoli. Scallops are particularly good with ingredients such as fresh ginger and soy sauce.

Serves 4
15ml/1 tbsp stir-fry oil or
  sunflower oil
500g/1¹/₄lb raw tiger prawns
  (jumbo shrimp), peeled
1 star anise
225g/8oz scallops, halved
  horizontally if large
2.5cm/1in piece fresh root ginger,
  peeled and grated
2 garlic cloves, thinly sliced
1 red (bell) pepper, seeded and
  cut into thin strips
115g/4oz/1³/₄ cups shiitake or
  button (white) mushrooms,
  thinly sliced
juice of 1 lemon
5ml/1 tsp cornflour (cornstarch),
  mixed to a paste with
  30ml/2 tbsp cold water
30ml/2 tbsp light soy sauce
salt and ground black pepper
chopped fresh chives, to garnish

1 Heat the oil in a wok until very hot. Put in the prawns and star anise and stir-fry over a high heat for 2 minutes.

2 Add the scallops, ginger and garlic and stir-fry for 1 minute more, by which time the prawns should have turned pink and the scallops will be opaque. Season with a little salt and plenty of pepper and then remove the prawns from the wok using a slotted spoon. Transfer the scallops to a bowl and discard the star anise.

3 Add the red pepper and mushrooms to the wok and stir-fry for 1–2 minutes. Pour in the lemon juice, cornflour paste and soy sauce, bring to the boil and bubble this mixture for 1–2 minutes, stirring all the time, until the sauce is smooth and slightly thickened.

4 Stir the prawns and scallops into the sauce, cook for a few seconds until heated through, then season with salt and ground black pepper. Spoon on to individual plates and serve garnished with the chives.

Scallops with Fennel Energy 362kcal/1512kJ; Protein 36.9g; Carbohydrate 9g, of which sugars 5.4g; Fat 20.1g, of which saturates 9.4g; Cholesterol 99mg; Calcium 79mg; Fibre 4.8g; Sodium 675mg.
Scallops and Prawns Energy 212kcal/892kJ; Protein 36.3g; Carbohydrate 6.6g, of which sugars 3.3g; Fat 4.6g, of which saturates 0.8g; Cholesterol 270mg; Calcium 122mg; Fibre 1g; Sodium 877mg.

Steamed Scallops with Ginger

It helps to have two woks when making this dish. Borrow an extra one from a friend, or use a large, heavy pan with a trivet for steaming the second plate of scallops. Take care not to overcook the tender seafood.

Serves 4

24 king scallops in their shells, cleaned
15ml/1 tbsp very finely shredded fresh root ginger
5ml/1 tsp very finely chopped garlic
1 large fresh red chilli, seeded and very finely chopped
15ml/1 tbsp light soy sauce
15ml/1 tbsp Chinese rice wine
a few drops of sesame oil
2–3 spring onions (scallions), very finely shredded
15ml/1 tbsp very finely chopped fresh chives
noodles or rice, to serve

1 Remove the scallops from their shells, then remove the membrane and hard white muscle from each one. Arrange the scallops on two plates. Rinse the shells, dry and set aside.

2 Fill two woks with 5cm/2in water and place a trivet in the base of each one. Bring to the boil.

3 Meanwhile, mix together the ginger, garlic, chilli, soy sauce, rice wine, sesame oil, spring onions and chives.

4 Spoon the flavourings over the scallops. Lower a plate into each of the woks. Turn the heat to low, cover and steam for 10–12 minutes.

5 Divide the scallops among four, or eight, of the reserved shells and serve immediately with noodles or rice.

Cook's Tip
Use the freshest scallops you can find. If you ask your fishmonger to shuck them, remember to ask for the shells so that you can use them for serving the scallops.

Spiced Scallops and Sugar Snaps

This is a great dish for special-occasion entertaining.

Serves 4

45ml/3 tbsp oyster sauce
10ml/2 tsp soy sauce
5ml/1 tsp sesame oil
5ml/1 tsp golden caster (superfine) sugar
30ml/2 tbsp sunflower oil
2 fresh red chillies, finely sliced
4 garlic cloves, finely chopped
10ml/2 tsp finely chopped fresh root ginger
250g/9oz sugar snap peas, trimmed
500g/1¼lb king scallops, cleaned and halved, roes discarded
3 spring onions (scallions), finely shredded

For the noodle cakes
250g/9oz fresh thin egg noodles
10ml/2 tsp sesame oil
120ml/4fl oz/½ cup sunflower oil

1 Cook the noodles in boiling water until tender. Drain, toss with the sesame oil and 15ml/1 tbsp of the sunflower oil and spread out on a large baking sheet. Leave to dry in a warm place for 1 hour.

2 Heat 15ml/1 tbsp of the sunflower oil in a wok. Add a quarter of the noodle mixture, flatten it and shape it into a cake.

3 Cook the cake for about 5 minutes on each side until crisp and golden. Drain on kitchen paper and keep hot while you make the remaining three noodle cakes in the same way.

4 Mix the oyster sauce, soy sauce, sesame oil and sugar, stirring until the sugar has dissolved completely.

5 Heat a wok, add the sunflower oil, then stir-fry the chillies, garlic, ginger and sugar snaps for 1–2 minutes. Add the scallops and spring onions and stir-fry for 1 minute, then add the sauce mixture and cook for 1 minute.

6 Place a noodle cake on each plate, top with the scallop mixture and serve immediately.

Spiced Scallops Energy 689kcal/2888kJ; Protein 41.4g; Carbohydrate 59.9g, of which sugars 6.2g; Fat 33.3g, of which saturates 5.4g; Cholesterol 78mg; Calcium 73mg; Fibre 5g; Sodium 700mg.
Scallops with Ginger Energy 392kcal/1621kJ; Protein 13.6g; Carbohydrate 4.5g, of which sugars 2.5g; Fat 34.1g, of which saturates 22.4g; Cholesterol 115mg; Calcium 63mg; Fibre 0.4g; Sodium 168mg.

Roasted Chicken with Grapes and Fresh Root Ginger

Oven-roasted chicken with a delicious blend of spices and sweet autumn fruit.

Serves 4

115–130g/4–4½oz fresh root ginger, grated
6–8 garlic cloves, roughly chopped
juice of 1 lemon
about 30ml/2 tbsp olive oil

2–3 large pinches of ground cinnamon
1–1.6kg/2¼–3½lb chicken
500g/1¼lb seeded red and green grapes
500g/1¼lb seedless green grapes
5–7 shallots, chopped
about 250ml/8fl oz/1 cup chicken stock
salt and ground black pepper

1 Mix together half the ginger, the garlic, half the lemon juice, the oil, cinnamon and seasoning. Rub over the chicken and set aside.

2 Meanwhile, cut the red and green seeded grapes in half, remove the seeds and set aside. Add the whole green seedless grapes to the halved ones.

3 Preheat the oven to 180°C/350°F/Gas 4. Heat a heavy frying pan or flameproof casserole until hot. Remove the chicken from the marinade and cook in the pan until browned on all sides.

4 Put a few shallots into the chicken cavity with the garlic and ginger from the marinade and as many of the red and green grapes as will fit. Roast for 40–60 minutes, or until cooked.

5 Remove the chicken from the pan and keep warm. Pour off any oil from the pan, reserving any sediment in the base. Add the remaining shallots and cook for 5 minutes until softened.

6 Add half the remaining red and green grapes, the remaining ginger, the stock and any juices from the chicken and cook over medium-high heat until the grapes have reduced to a thick sauce. Season with salt, pepper and the remaining lemon juice.

7 Serve the chicken on a warmed serving dish, surrounded by the sauce and the reserved grapes.

Chicken and Mushroom Donburi

'Donburi' means a one-dish meal, and its name comes from the eponymous Japanese porcelain food bowl. This dish is ideal for using the mushrooms that are abundant in autumn.

Serves 4

10ml/2 tsp groundnut (peanut) oil
50g/2oz/4 tbsp butter
2 garlic cloves, crushed
2.5cm/1in piece of fresh root ginger, grated
5 spring onions, diagonally sliced
1 green chilli, seeded and sliced

3 skinless chicken breast fillets, cut into thin strips
150g/5oz tofu, cut into small cubes
115g/4oz/1¾ shiitake mushrooms, stalks discarded and cups sliced
15ml/1 tbsp Japanese rice wine
30ml/2 tbsp light soy sauce
10ml/2 tsp sugar
400ml/14fl oz/1⅔ cups hot chicken stock

For the rice
225–275g/8–10oz/generous 1–1½ cups Japanese rice or Thai fragrant rice

1 Cook the rice by the absorption method or by following the instructions on the packet.

2 While the rice is cooking, heat the oil and half the butter in a large frying pan. Stir-fry the garlic, ginger, spring onions and chilli for 1–2 minutes until slightly softened. Add the strips of chicken and fry, in batches if necessary, until all the pieces are browned.

3 Transfer the chicken mixture to a plate and add the tofu to the pan. Stir-fry for a few minutes, then add the mushrooms. Stir-fry for 2–3 minutes over a medium heat until the mushrooms are tender.

4 Stir in the rice wine, soy sauce and sugar and cook briskly for 1–2 minutes, stirring all the time. Return the chicken to the pan, toss over the heat for about 2 minutes, then pour in the stock. Stir well and cook over low heat for about 5–6 minutes until the stock is bubbling.

5 Spoon the rice into individual serving bowls and pile the chicken mixture on top, making sure that each portion gets a generous amount of chicken sauce.

Roasted Chicken Energy 454kcal/1891kJ; Protein 31.6g; Carbohydrate 19.5g, of which sugars 19.5g; Fat 28.1g, of which saturates 7.1g; Cholesterol 165mg; Calcium 28mg; Fibre 1g; Sodium 116mg.
Chicken Donburi Energy 408kcal/1709kJ; Protein 35.2g; Carbohydrate 46.3g, of which sugars 1.1g; Fat 8.8g, of which saturates 1.2g; Cholesterol 79mg; Calcium 216mg; Fibre 0.5g; Sodium 605mg.

Coq au Vin

This rustic, one-pot casserole contains chunky pieces of chicken, slowly simmered in a rich red wine sauce until tender, making it a welcome meal on a cold autumn's night.

Serves 6

45ml/3 tbsp light olive oil
12 shallots
225g/8oz rindless streaky (fatty)
   bacon rashers (strips), chopped
3 garlic cloves, finely chopped
225g/8oz small mushrooms, halved
6 boneless chicken thighs

3 chicken breast fillets, halved
1 bottle red wine
salt and ground black pepper
45ml/3 tbsp chopped fresh
   parsley, to garnish
boiled potatoes, to serve

For the bouquet garni
3 sprigs each parsley, thyme, sage
1 bay leaf
4 peppercorns

For the beurre manié
25g/1oz/2 tbsp butter, softened
25g/1oz/¼ cup plain
   (all-purpose) flour

1 Heat the oil in a flameproof casserole and cook the shallots for 5 minutes until golden. Increase the heat, then add the bacon, garlic and mushrooms and cook, stirring, for 10 minutes.

2 Transfer the cooked ingredients to a plate, then brown the chicken pieces in the oil remaining in the pan, turning them until golden brown all over. Return the shallots, garlic, mushrooms and bacon to the casserole and pour in the red wine.

3 Tie the ingredients for the bouquet garni in a bundle in a small piece of muslin (cheesecloth) and add to the casserole. Bring to the boil. Reduce the heat, cover and simmer for 30–40 minutes.

4 To make the beurre manié, cream the butter and flour together in a bowl using your fingers to make a smooth paste. Add small lumps of the paste to the casserole, stirring well until each piece has melted. When all the paste has been added, bring the casserole back to the boil and simmer for 5 minutes.

5 Season the casserole to taste with salt and pepper. Serve immediately, garnished with chopped fresh parsley and accompanied by boiled potatoes.

Chicken and Pork in Peanut Sauce

This traditional dish is made with dried potatoes, which break up when cooked to thicken the sauce. The same effect is achieved here by using floury potatoes, which are widely available in the autumn as the maincrop season hits full swing.

Serves 6

75g/3oz/¾ cup unsalted peanuts
60ml/4 tbsp olive oil
3 chicken breast portions, halved
500g/1¼lb boneless pork loin,
   cut into 2cm/¾in pieces

1 large onion, chopped
3 garlic cloves, crushed
5ml/1 tsp paprika
5ml/1 tsp ground cumin
500g/1¼lb floury potatoes,
   peeled and thickly sliced
550ml/18fl oz/scant 2½ cups
   vegetable stock
salt and ground black pepper
cooked rice, to serve

For the garnish
2 hard-boiled eggs, sliced
50g/2oz/½ cup pitted black olives
chopped fresh flat leaf parsley

1 Place the peanuts in a large dry frying pan over low heat. Toast for 2–3 minutes, until golden. Leave to cool, then process in a food processor until finely ground.

2 Heat half the oil in a heavy pan. Add the chicken pieces, season and cook for 10 minutes, until golden brown all over.

3 Transfer the pieces of chicken to a plate, using a slotted spoon. Heat the remaining oil and cook the pork for about 3–4 minutes, until brown. Transfer to the plate with the cooked chicken pieces.

4 Lower the heat, add the onion and fry for 5 minutes. Add the garlic, paprika and cumin and fry for 1 minute. Stir in the sliced potatoes, cover the pan and cook for a further 3 minutes. Mix in the peanuts and stock. Simmer for 30 minutes.

5 Return the meat to the pan and bring to the boil. Lower the heat, replace the lid and simmer for 6–8 minutes.

6 Garnish the stew with the egg slices, black olives and chopped parsley. Serve with the rice.

Coq au Vin Energy 538kcal/2240kJ; Protein 43.5g; Carbohydrate 7g, of which sugars 2.8g; Fat 28.2g, of which saturates 8.9g; Cholesterol 170mg; Calcium 50mg; Fibre 1.1g; Sodium 610mg.
Chicken in Peanut Sauce Energy 394kcal/1651kJ; Protein 39.3g; Carbohydrate 16.7g, of which sugars 2.4g; Fat 19.4g, of which saturates 4.1g; Cholesterol 85mg; Calcium 33mg; Fibre 1.8g; Sodium 123mg.

Hunter's Stew

Hearty and sustaining, this cabbage and meat stew is an ideal dish as the autumn nights get longer.

Serves 6–8
1kg/2¼lb fresh cabbage, shredded
10 dried mushrooms
2 onions, chopped
500g/1¼lb smoked sausage, sliced
1kg/2¼lb sauerkraut, drained
2 cooking apples, peeled, cored and diced
10 prunes
10 juniper berries, crushed

3–4 bay leaves
10 peppercorns
2.5ml/½ tsp salt
750ml/1¼ pints/3 cups boiling water
500g/1¼lb roast pork, diced
500g/1¼lb roast beef, diced
500g/1¼lb boiled ham, diced
150ml/¼ pint/⅔ cup dry red wine
5ml/1 tsp honey
wholemeal (whole-wheat) or rye bread and chilled vodka, to serve

1 Place the cabbage in a heatproof colander and wilt the leaves by carefully pouring boiling water over them. Rinse the mushrooms, then place them in a bowl with enough warm water to cover. Leave to soak for 15 minutes, then transfer to a pan and cook in the soaking liquid for 30 minutes. Strain, reserving the cooking liquid, then cut the mushrooms into strips.

2 Put the onions and smoked sausage in a small frying pan and fry gently, until the onions have softened. Remove the sausage from the pan and set aside.

3 Put the wilted cabbage and drained sauerkraut in a large pan, then add the cooked onions, along with the mushrooms, mushroom cooking liquid, apples, prunes, juniper berries, bay leaves, peppercorns and salt. Pour over the boiling water, then cover and simmer gently for 1 hour.

4 Add the cooked sausage to the pan with the other cooked, diced meats. Pour in the wine and add the honey. Cook, uncovered, for a further 40 minutes, stirring frequently. Adjust the seasoning as required. Remove from the heat. Allow to cool, then cover it and chill overnight. Simmer for 10 minutes to heat through before serving with bread and a glass of vodka.

Stuffed Cabbage Leaves

This is a great dish for making in the autumn when cabbages are at their peak. The leaves are stuffed with delicious beef and then baked in a tomato sauce.

Serves 6–8
1kg/2¼lb lean minced (ground) beef
75g/3oz/scant ½ cup long grain rice
4 onions, 2 chopped and 2 sliced

5–8 garlic cloves, chopped
2 eggs
45ml/3 tbsp water
1 large head of white or green cabbage
2 x 400g/14oz cans chopped tomatoes
45ml/3 tbsp demerara (raw) sugar
45ml/3 tbsp white wine vinegar, cider vinegar or lemon juice
pinch of ground cinnamon
salt and ground black pepper
lemon wedges, to serve

1 Put the beef, rice, 5ml/1 tsp salt, pepper, chopped onions and garlic in a bowl. Beat the eggs with the water, and combine with the meat mixture. Chill in the refrigerator until needed.

2 Cut the core from the cabbage in a cone shape and discard. Bring a large pan of water to the boil, lower the cabbage into the water and blanch for 1–2 minutes, then remove from the pan. Peel one or two layers of leaves off, then re-submerge the cabbage. Repeat until all the leaves are removed.

3 Preheat the oven to 150°C/300°F/Gas 2. Form the beef mixture into ovals, the size of small lemons, and wrap each in one or two cabbage leaves, folding and overlapping the leaves so that the mixture is completely enclosed.

4 Lay the cabbage rolls in the base of a large ovenproof dish, alternating with the sliced onions. Pour the tomatoes over and add the sugar, vinegar or lemon juice, salt, pepper and cinnamon. Cover and bake for 2 hours.

5 During cooking, remove the parcels from the oven and baste them with the tomato juices two or three times. After 2 hours, uncover the dish and cook for a further 30–60 minutes, or until the tomato sauce has thickened and is lightly browned on top. Serve hot with wedges of lemon.

Hunter's Stew Energy 546kcal/2279kJ; Protein 50.4g; Carbohydrate 24.6g, of which sugars 19.8g; Fat 26.4g, of which saturates 9.7g; Cholesterol 149mg; Calcium 213mg; Fibre 7.7g; Sodium 2122mg.
Stuffed Cabbage Energy 425kcal/1773kJ; Protein 29.7g; Carbohydrate 27.5g, of which sugars 17.6g; Fat 22.3g, of which saturates 9.2g; Cholesterol 123mg; Calcium 86mg; Fibre 3.7g; Sodium 134mg.

Steak and Mushroom Pudding with a Herby Suet Crust

This dish can seem like a lot of work, but the results are heaven on an autumn night.

Serves 6
25g/1oz/^{1}/$_2$ cup dried porcini mushrooms, soaked in warm water for 20 minutes
1.3kg/3lb rump (round) steak
30ml/2 tbsp plain (all-purpose) flour
30ml/2 tbsp olive or sunflower oil
1 large onion, chopped
225g/8oz chestnut or open cup mushrooms, halved if large
300ml/^{1}/$_2$ pint/1^1/$_4$ cups red wine
300ml/^{1}/$_2$ pint/1^1/$_4$ cups beef stock
45ml/3 tbsp mushroom ketchup
1 bay leaf

For the herby suet crust
275g/10oz/2^1/$_2$ cups self-raising (self-rising) flour
5ml/1 tsp baking powder
15ml/1 tbsp each finely chopped fresh parsley, sage, rosemary and thyme
finely grated rind of 1 lemon
75g/3oz/1^1/$_2$ cups beef or vegetable suet (US chilled, grated shortening)
50g/2oz/^{1}/$_4$ cup butter, chilled and grated
1 egg, beaten
juice of ^{1}/$_2$ lemon
150ml/^{1}/$_4$ pint/^{2}/$_3$ cup cold water
salt and ground black pepper

1 Preheat the oven to 180°C/350°F/Gas 4. Drain the porcini mushrooms, reserving the soaking liquid, and roughly chop. Cut the steak into large cubes, then toss with the flour and seasoning.

2 Heat the oil in a large frying pan until very hot. Add the onion and cook, stirring frequently until golden brown. Using a slotted spoon, transfer the onions to an ovenproof casserole. Fry the floured steak in batches until well browned on all sides.

3 Add the meat to the casserole with all the mushrooms. Pour in the reserved soaking liquid, wine and stock, add the ketchup, if using, and the bay leaf. Cover and cook for 1^1/$_2$ hours, until the meat is tender. Allow the mixture to cool completely.

4 To make the crust, butter a deep 1.7 litre/3 pint/7 cup ovenproof bowl. Sift the flour, baking powder and 2.5ml/^{1}/$_2$ tsp salt into a large mixing bowl. Stir in the herbs and lemon rind and season with pepper. Stir in the suet and butter. Make a well in the centre, add the egg, lemon juice and enough of the cold water to mix and gather into a soft but manageable dough.

5 Knead the dough lightly on a well-floured work surface. Cut off a quarter of the dough and wrap in cling film (plastic wrap). Shape the rest into a ball and roll out into a large round, big enough to line the bowl. Lift up the dough and drop it into the bowl, pressing against the sides to line the bowl evenly. Roll out the reserved pastry to a round large enough to use as a lid.

6 Spoon in the beef filling to within 1cm/^{1}/$_2$in of the rim. Top up with the gravy. (Keep the rest to serve with the pudding later.) Dampen the edges of the pastry and fit the lid. Press the edges to seal and trim away the excess. Cover with pleated, buttered baking parchment, then with pleated foil. Tie string under the lip of the basin to hold the paper in place, then take it over the top to form a handle. Place in a large pan of simmering water, cover and steam for 1^1/$_2$ hours, topping up with boiling water as necessary. Bring the bowl to the table to serve.

Beef with Chanterelle Mushrooms in a Cream Sauce

The trick here is to use really good beef with no fat and to fry the dried pieces quickly in the hot oil so the outside is well browned and the inside very rare. Chanterelle mushrooms are the most delicious wild mushrooms, yellowy orange in colour and with a shape like inverted umbrellas. Enjoy them throughout the autumn months.

Serves 4
115g/4oz chanterelle mushrooms
2 rump (round) steaks, 175g/6oz each, cut into strips
45ml/3 tbsp olive oil
1 garlic clove, crushed
1 shallot, finely chopped
60ml/4 tbsp dry white wine
60ml/4 tbsp double (heavy) cream
25g/1oz/2 tbsp butter
salt and ground black pepper
chopped fresh parsley, to garnish

1 Clean the mushrooms. If you have collected them from the wild, cut off the ends where they have come from the ground and, using kitchen paper, wipe off any leaf matter or moss. Trim the mushrooms, then halve them through the stalk and cap.

2 Dry the beef thoroughly on kitchen paper. Heat a large frying pan over a high heat, then add 30ml/2 tbsp olive oil. Working in batches, add the meat to the hot oil in the pan and quickly brown the strips on all sides.

3 Remove the meat, which should still be very rare, from the pan, set aside and keep warm. Add the remaining olive oil to the pan and reduce the heat. Stir in the garlic and shallot and cook, stirring, for about 1 minute.

4 Increase the heat and add the mushrooms. Season and cook until they start to soften. Add the wine, bring to the boil and add the cream. As the liquid thickens, return the beef to the pan and heat through.

5 Remove the pan from the heat and swirl in the butter. Serve on warmed plates, garnished with the parsley.

Fig and Walnut Torte

This recipe is a sweet, comforting treat for the autumn months.

Makes 20–25 pieces
75g/3oz/⅓ cup butter, melted, plus extra for greasing
175g/6oz/1½ cups walnuts, finely chopped
115g/4oz/1 cup ground almonds
75g/3oz/⅓ cup caster (superfine) sugar
10ml/2 tsp ground cinnamon

9 sheets of filo pastry, thawed if frozen, each cut into two 30 x 20cm/12 x 8in rectangles
4 fresh figs, sliced
Greek (US strained plain) yogurt, to serve

For the syrup
350g/12oz/1½ cups caster (superfine) sugar
4 whole cloves
1 cinnamon stick
2 strips of lemon rind

1 Preheat the oven to 160°C/325°F/Gas 3. Grease a 30 × 20cm/12 × 8in shallow baking tin (pan) with melted butter. Mix the walnuts, ground almonds, sugar and cinnamon and set aside.

2 Fit a sheet of filo pastry in the base of the tin. Brush with some melted butter and place a sheet of filo on top. Repeat this until you have layered up eight sheets. Spoon half the nut mixture over the pastry to the edges, and top with the fig slices. Place two filo sheets on top of the figs, brushing each with more melted butter as before, then evenly spoon over the remaining nut mixture.

3 Layer the remaining filo sheets on top, buttering each one. Brush melted butter over the top of the torte, then score the surface in a diamond pattern. Bake for 1 hour until golden.

4 Meanwhile, make the syrup. Place all the ingredients in a pan and mix well. Heat, stirring, until the sugar has dissolved. Bring to the boil, lower the heat and simmer for 10 minutes until syrupy, stirring occasionally.

5 Allow the syrup to cool for about 15 minutes, then strain it evenly over the hot torte. Allow to cool and leave to soak for 2–3 hours, then cut the torte into diamonds or squares and serve with Greek yogurt.

Papaya Baked with Ginger

Ginger enhances the flavour of papaya in this recipe, which takes no more than ten minutes to prepare. Don't overcook the papaya or the flesh will become very watery.

Serves 4
2 ripe papayas
2 pieces stem ginger in syrup, drained, plus 15ml/1 tbsp syrup from the jar

8 amaretti or other dessert biscuits (cookies), coarsely crushed
45ml/3 tbsp raisins
shredded, finely pared rind and juice of 1 lime
25g/1oz/¼ cup pistachio nuts, chopped
15ml/1 tbsp light muscovado (brown) sugar
60ml/4 tbsp crème fraîche, plus extra to serve

1 Preheat the oven to 200°C/400°F/Gas 6. Cut the papayas in half and scoop out their seeds. Place the halves in a baking dish and set aside. Cut the stem ginger into fine matchsticks.

2 Make the filling. Combine the crushed amaretti biscuits, stem ginger matchsticks and raisins in a bowl. Stir in the lime rind and juice, two-thirds of the nuts, then add the sugar and the crème fraîche. Mix well.

3 Fill the papaya halves and drizzle with the ginger syrup. Sprinkle with the remaining nuts. Bake for about 25 minutes or until tender. Serve with extra crème fraîche.

Cook's Tip
If crème fraîche is not available, make your own version. Combine 250ml/8fl oz/1 cup whipping cream and 30ml/2 tbsp buttermilk in a glass bowl. Cover at room temperature for 8 to 24 hours, or until thick. Stir well, cover and refrigerate for up to 10 days.

Variation
You can use almonds or walnuts instead of pistachio nuts.

Fig Torte Energy 218kcal/915kJ; Protein 3.5g; Carbohydrate 29.2g, of which sugars 22.2g; Fat 10.5g, of which saturates 2.3g; Cholesterol 15mg; Calcium 59mg; Fibre 1.4g; Sodium 32mg.
Papaya with Ginger Energy 292kcal/1228kJ; Protein 3.6g; Carbohydrate 44.6g, of which sugars 35.7g; Fat 12.3g, of which saturates 5.7g; Cholesterol 17mg; Calcium 84mg; Fibre 4.2g; Sodium 127mg.

Butternut Squash and Maple Pie

This American-style autumn
pie has a crisp pastry case
and a creamy filling,
sweetened with maple syrup
and flavoured with fresh
ginger and a dash of brandy.

Serves 10

1 small butternut squash
60ml/4 tbsp water
2.5cm/1in piece fresh root ginger,
  peeled and grated

275g/10oz shortcrust pastry
120ml/4fl oz/½ cup double
  (heavy) cream
90ml/6 tbsp maple syrup
40g/1½oz/3 tbsp light
  muscovado (brown) sugar
3 eggs, lightly beaten
30ml/2 tbsp brandy
1.5ml/¼ tsp grated nutmeg
beaten egg, to glaze

1 Halve the squash, peel and scoop out the seeds. Cut the
flesh into cubes and put in a pan with the water. Cover and
cook gently for 15 minutes. Uncover, stir in the ginger and cook
for a further 5 minutes until the liquid has evaporated and the
squash is tender. Cool slightly, then purée in a food processor.

2 Roll out the pastry and use to line a 23cm/9in flan tin (pan).
Re-roll the trimmings, then cut into maple leaf shapes. Brush the
edge of the pastry case with beaten egg and attach the leaf
shapes at regular intervals to make a decorative rim. Cover
with clear film (plastic wrap) and chill for 30 minutes.

3 Put a heavy baking sheet in the oven and preheat to 200°C/
400°F/Gas 6. Prick the pastry base, line with foil and fill with
baking beans. Bake blind on the baking sheet for 12 minutes.

4 Remove the foil and beans and bake for a further 5 minutes.
Brush the base of the pastry case with beaten egg and return
to the oven for about 3 minutes. Lower the oven temperature
to 180°C/350°F/Gas 4.

5 Mix 200g/7oz/scant 1 cup of the butternut purée with the
cream, syrup, sugar, eggs, brandy and nutmeg. (Discard any
remaining purée.) Pour into the pastry case. Bake for about
30 minutes, until the filling is lightly set. Leave to cool slightly
and serve immediately.

Blackberry Ice Cream

There could scarcely be
fewer ingredients in this
delicious, vibrant ice cream.
Blackberries are a feature of
early autumn and can often
be picked wild on hedges at
the side of roads and
country paths. Use store-
bought cookies or make
your own.

Serves 4–6

500g/1¼lb/5 cups blackberries,
  hulled, plus extra, to decorate
75g/3oz/6 tbsp caster
  (superfine) sugar
30ml/2 tbsp water
300ml/½ pint/1¼ cups
  whipping cream
crisp dessert biscuits (cookies),
  to serve

1 Put the blackberries into a pan, and add the sugar and water.
Cover and simmer for 5 minutes until just soft. Place the fruit
in a sieve (strainer) over a bowl and press it through using a
wooden spoon. Leave to cool, then chill.

2 BY HAND: Whip the cream until it is just thick but still soft
enough to fall from a spoon, then mix it with the chilled
fruit purée. Pour the mixture into a plastic tub or similar
freezerproof container and freeze for 2 hours.
USING AN ICE CREAM MAKER: Churn the chilled purée for
10–15 minutes until it is thick, then gradually pour in the
cream. There is no need to whip the cream first.

3 BY HAND: Mash the mixture with a fork, or beat it in a food
processor to break up the ice crystals. Return it to the freezer
for 4 hours more, beating the mixture again after 2 hours.
USING AN ICE CREAM MAKER: Continue to churn the ice cream
until it is firm enough to scoop.

4 Scoop into dishes and decorate with extra blackberries.
Serve with crisp dessert biscuits.

Variation
• Frozen blackberries can be used for the purée. You will
  need to increase the cooking time to 10 minutes.
• Blackcurrants can be used instead of blackberries.

Butternut Pie Energy 266kcal/1109kJ; Protein 4g; Carbohydrate 26.2g, of which sugars 13.7g; Fat 16.1g, of which saturates 4.6g; Cholesterol 74mg; Calcium 56mg; Fibre 1.4g; Sodium 92mg.
Blackberry Ice Energy 261kcal/1081kJ; Protein 1.8g; Carbohydrate 18.7g, of which sugars 18.7g; Fat 20.3g, of which saturates 12.6g; Cholesterol 53mg; Calcium 70mg; Fibre 2.6g; Sodium 15mg.

Figs and Pears in Honey with Cardamom

Fresh figs picked straight from the tree are so delicious that it seems almost sacrilege to cook them – unless you have so many during the fruit's season that you fancy a change – when you can try this superb recipe.

Serves 4
1 lemon
90ml/6 tbsp clear honey
1 cinnamon stick
1 cardamom pod
350ml/12fl oz/1½ cups water
2 pears
8 fresh figs, halved

1 Pare the rind from the lemon using a cannelle knife (zester) or vegetable peeler and cut the rind into very thin strips.

2 Place the lemon rind, honey, cinnamon stick, cardamom pod and the water in a pan and boil, uncovered, for about 10 minutes, until the liquid is reduced by about half.

3 Cut the pears into eighths, discarding the core. Leave the peel on or discard, as preferred.

4 Place the pear pieces in the syrup; add the figs. Bring the mixture to just near boiling point, then reduce the heat and simmer for about 5 minutes, until the fruit is tender.

5 Transfer the fruit from the pan to a serving bowl with a slotted spoon. Cook the liquid until syrupy, discard the cinnamon stick and pour the sauce over the figs and pears. Serve warm or cold.

Cook's Tip
The season for fresh figs reaches its peak in September and October, so make this dish earlier in the autumn rather than later. Figs are extremely perishable and should be used as soon after purchase as possible. Store fresh figs in the refrigerator for about 2 to 3 days.

Honey Baked Figs with Hazelnut Ice Cream

Figs baked in a lemon grass-scented honey syrup have the most wonderful flavour, especially when served with a good-quality ice cream dotted with roasted hazelnuts. If you prefer to avoid nuts, because you don't like them or because a guest has an allergy, use plain rich vanilla or toffee ice cream instead.

Serves 4
1 lemon grass stalk,
   finely chopped
1 cinnamon stick, roughly broken
60ml/4 tbsp clear honey
200ml/7fl oz/scant 1 cup water
75g/3oz/¾ cup hazelnuts
8 large ripe dessert figs
400ml/14fl oz/1⅔ cups
   good-quality vanilla ice cream
30ml/2 tbsp hazelnut
   liqueur (optional)

1 Preheat the oven to 190°C/375°F/Gas 5. Make the syrup by mixing the lemon grass, cinnamon stick, honey and measured water in a small pan. Heat gently, stirring until the honey has dissolved, then bring to the boil. Simmer for 2 minutes.

2 Meanwhile, spread out the hazelnuts on a baking sheet and grill (broil) under medium heat until golden brown. Shake the sheet occasionally, so that they are evenly toasted.

3 Cut the figs into quarters, leaving them intact at the bases. Stand the figs in a baking dish and pour the syrup over. Cover the dish tightly with foil and bake for 13–15 minutes until the figs are tender.

4 While the figs are baking, remove the ice cream from the freezer and let it soften slightly. Chop the hazelnuts roughly and beat the softened ice cream briefly with an electric beater, then fold in the toasted hazelnuts until evenly distributed.

5 To serve, puddle a little of the syrup from the figs on to each individual dessert plate. Arrange the figs on top and add a spoonful of the nutty ice cream. At the very last moment before serving, spoon a little hazelnut liqueur over the ice cream, if you like.

Figs and Pears Energy 143kcal/606kJ; Protein 1.7g; Carbohydrate 34.4g, of which sugars 34.4g; Fat 0.7g, of which saturates 0g; Cholesterol 0mg; Calcium 109mg; Fibre 4.7g; Sodium 28mg.
Honey Baked Figs Energy 433kcal/1816kJ; Protein 7.8g; Carbohydrate 53.6g, of which sugars 52.1g; Fat 21.2g, of which saturates 7g; Cholesterol 24mg; Calcium 227mg; Fibre 4.2g; Sodium 88mg.

Cinnamon Squash

Lightly cooked butternut squash makes a delicious smoothie. It has a wonderfully rich, rounded flavour that is lifted perfectly by the addition of tart citrus juice and warm, spicy cinnamon. Imagine pumpkin pie as a gorgeous smooth drink and you're halfway to experiencing the flavours of this lusciously sweet and tantalizing treat.

Serves 2–3

1 small butternut squash, total weight about 600g/1lb 6oz
2.5ml/½ tsp ground cinnamon
3 large lemons
1 grapefruit
60ml/4 tbsp light muscovado (brown) sugar
ice cubes

1 Cut the squash in half, scoop out the seeds using a spoon and discard. Cut the flesh into chunks. Using a sharp knife, cut away the skin and discard.

2 Steam or boil the squash for 10–15 minutes until just tender. Drain well and leave to stand until cool.

3 Put the cooled squash in a blender or food processor and add the ground cinnamon.

4 Squeeze the lemons and grapefruit and pour the juice over the squash, then add the muscovado sugar.

5 Process the ingredients until they are smooth. If necessary, pause to scrape down the side of the processor or blender.

6 Put a few ice cubes in two or three short glasses and pour over the smoothie. Serve immediately.

Cook's Tip

If you can only buy a large squash, cook it all and add the leftovers to stew or soup.

Sweet Dream

A soothing blend guaranteed to wake you up slowly, this fruity threesome is naturally sweet so there is no need for any additional sugar. Fresh grapefruit juice marries brilliantly with the dried fruits, and rich creamy yogurt makes a delicious contrast of colour and flavour – simply perfect to sip over a leisurely breakfast while reading the newspaper.

Serves 2

25g/1oz/scant ¼ cup dried figs or dates, stoned (pitted)
50g/2oz/¼ cup ready-to-eat prunes
25g/1oz/scant ¼ cup sultanas (golden raisins)
1 grapefruit
350ml/12fl oz/1½ cups full cream (whole) milk
30ml/2 tbsp Greek (US strained plain) yogurt

1 Put the dried fruits in a blender or food processor. Squeeze out the grapefruit juice and add to the machine. Blend until smooth, scraping the mixture down from the side of the bowl, if necessary.

2 Pour the milk into the blender or processor. Blend the mixture until it is completely smooth, scraping down the sides as before.

3 Using a teaspoon, tap a spoonful of the yogurt around the inside of each of two tall glasses so that it runs up in a spiral pattern – don't worry if it isn't too neat. Pour in the fruit mixture and serve immediately.

Variations

• *To make a dairy-free version of this drink, omit the Greek (US strained plain) yogurt and use soya or rice milk instead of ordinary milk. The consistency of the smoothie will not be as creamy but it will still be delicious – and perhaps better for those who prefer a lighter drink in the morning. It will also be drinkable by those on a dairy-free diet.*
• *Other dried fruits can be used as well: try raisins, currants or ready-to-eat dried apricots.*

Cinnamon Squash Energy 121kcal/513kJ; Protein 1.9g; Carbohydrate 28.9g, of which sugars 27.9g; Fat 0.5g, of which saturates 0.2g; Cholesterol 0mg; Calcium 81mg; Fibre 2.7g; Sodium 3mg.
Sweet Dream Energy 246kcal/1033kJ; Protein 8.6g; Carbohydrate 38.3g, of which sugars 38.3g; Fat 7.4g, of which saturates 4.5g; Cholesterol 25mg; Calcium 301mg; Fibre 3.7g; Sodium 103mg.

Smoked Haddock Chowder

Based on a traditional Scottish recipe, this soup combines the sweetness of sweet potatoes and butternut squash with aromatic Thai basil.

Serves 6

400g/14oz sweet potatoes (pink-fleshed variety), diced
225g/8oz peeled butternut squash, cut into 1cm/½in slices

50g/2oz/¼ cup butter
1 onion, chopped
450g/1lb Finnan haddock fillets, skinned
300ml/½ pint/1¼ cups water
600ml/1 pint/2½ cups milk
small handful of Thai basil leaves
60ml/4 tbsp double (heavy) cream
salt and ground black pepper

1 Cook the sweet potatoes and butternut squash separately in a large pan of boiling salted water for 15 minutes or until tender. Drain well.

2 Meanwhile, melt half the butter in a large, heavy pan. Add the onion and cook for 4–5 minutes, until softened but not browned. Add the haddock fillets and water.

3 Bring to the boil, reduce the heat and simmer for 10 minutes, until the fish is cooked. Use a draining spoon to lift the fish out of the pan and leave to cool. Set the liquid aside.

4 When cool enough to handle, carefully break the flesh into large flakes, discarding the skin and bones. Set the fish aside.

5 Press the sweet potatoes through a sieve (strainer) and beat in the remaining butter with seasoning to taste.

6 Strain the reserved fish cooking liquid and return it to the rinsed-out pan, then whisk in the sweet potato. Stir in the milk and bring to the boil. Simmer for about 2–3 minutes.

7 Stir the butternut squash, fish, Thai basil leaves and cream into the soup. Season the soup to taste and heat through without boiling. Ladle the soup into six warmed soup bowls and serve immediately.

Chicken Soup

This versatile chicken soup should be an essential part of every cook's winter repertoire. In this version, a rich stock is prepared using a whole chicken.

Serves 8–10

1 chicken, about 2kg/4½lb
350g/12oz beef bone
2 bay leaves
3 large leeks, sliced
1 parsnip, thinly sliced

4 carrots, thinly sliced
6 celery sticks, sliced
salt
75ml/5 tbsp chopped fresh parsley, to garnish

For the dumplings

350g/12oz/3 cups plain (all-purpose) flour
125g/4oz/½ cup butter
4 eggs
5ml/1 tsp sugar
salt

1 Bring 3 litres/5 pints/12½ cups water to the boil in a large pan. Add the chicken, beef bone and bay leaves to the pot, and return to the boil. Skim, lower the heat and simmer for 1 hour.

2 Add the leeks, parsnip, carrots and celery to the chicken stock and season with salt. Simmer for about 20 minutes, until the vegetables are tender.

3 Meanwhile, make the dumplings. Place the flour in a bowl. Bring 250ml/8fl oz/1 cup water to the boil in a pan, add the butter and return to the boil. Stir the mixture into the flour, beating vigorously with a fork to blend smoothly. Leave to cool.

4 Beat in the eggs, one at a time, to make a soft dough. Stir in the sugar and salt to taste. Leave to rest for 20 minutes.

5 Bring a large pan of lightly salted water to the boil. Use a teaspoon to form small, unevenly shaped balls of dough, and drop them one at a time into the water. They will sink to the bottom, then rise to the top when cooked, in 3–5 minutes. Lift out the dumplings and set aside until needed.

6 Remove the beef bone from the soup. Carve the chicken to serve separately, or pull the meat from the bones and return to the soup. Add the dumplings to warm through, and serve.

Haddock Chowder Energy 285kcal/1196kJ; Protein 19.1g; Carbohydrate 20.7g, of which sugars 9.9g; Fat 14.7g, of which saturates 8.9g; Cholesterol 64mg; Calcium 166mg; Fibre 2.1g; Sodium 173mg.
Chicken Soup Energy 266kcal/1115kJ; Protein 25.7g; Carbohydrate 24g, of which sugars 6.6g; Fat 7.5g, of which saturates 1.2g; Cholesterol 109mg; Calcium 48mg; Fibre 2.7g; Sodium 86mg.

Kale, Chorizo and Potato Soup

This hearty winter soup has a spicy kick from the chorizo sausage. The soup becomes more potent if chilled overnight. It is worth buying the best possible chorizo sausage to achieve superior flavour.

Serves 6–8

225g/8oz kale, stems removed
225g/8oz chorizo sausage
675g/1½lb potatoes, cut
 into chunks
1.75 litres/3 pints/7½ cups
 vegetable stock
5ml/1 tsp ground black pepper
pinch of cayenne pepper (optional)
12 slices French bread, toasted on
 both sides
salt and ground black pepper

1 Place the kale in a food processor or blender and process for a few seconds to chop it finely. Alternatively, shred it finely by hand.

2 Prick the sausages and place in a pan with enough water to cover. Bring just to boiling point, then reduce the heat immediately before the water boils too rapidly and simmer for 15 minutes. Drain and cut into thin slices.

3 Boil the potatoes for about 15 minutes or until the slices are just tender. Drain, and place in a bowl, then mash adding a little of the cooking liquid to form a thick paste.

4 Bring the vegetable stock to the boil and add the kale. Bring back to the boil. Reduce the heat and add the chorizo, then simmer for 5 minutes. Gradually add the potato paste, stirring it into the soup, then simmer for 20 minutes. Season with black pepper and cayenne.

5 Divide the freshly made toast among serving bowls. Pour the soup over and serve immediately, sprinkled with pepper.

> **Cook's Tip**
> *Select seasonal maincrop, floury potatoes for this soup rather than new potatoes or waxy salad potatoes.*

Hare Soup

This soup can be made with any other game that is available in the winter months, such as wild duck, goose or guinea fowl.

Serves 6

1 hare or rabbit
2 carrots
75ml/5 tbsp olive oil
75ml/5 tbsp dry white port
1 onion, sliced
1 leek, sliced
1 garlic clove, chopped
6 black peppercorns
1 bay leaf
15ml/1 tbsp cornflour
 (cornstarch)
1 turnip, diced
3 heads pak choi (bok choy), cut
 into strips
200g/7oz oyster
 mushrooms, sliced
300g/11oz/2¼ cups cooked
 haricot (navy) beans
1 small bunch of fresh
 peppermint, chopped
salt

1 Cut the hare into pieces. Wash well and pat dry with kitchen paper. Slice one carrot and dice the other. Heat 45ml/3 tbsp of the oil in a large pan. Add the pieces of hare and cook, turning occasionally, for about 10 minutes, until golden brown all over.

2 Drain off the oil from the pan. Add the port, onion, leek, sliced carrot, garlic, peppercorns and bay leaf, and pour in enough water to cover. Bring to the boil, then lower the heat and simmer gently for 1½ hours.

3 Strain the stock into a bowl and reserve the meat. Remove the bones from the meat and cut the meat into small pieces. Return the stock to the rinsed-out pan and set over a low heat.

4 Mix the cornflour to a paste with 30ml/2 tbsp water. Stir it into the stock and season to taste with salt.

5 Cook the remaining carrot, the turnip and pak choi in separate pans of boiling water until just tender, then add to the stock.

6 Meanwhile, heat the remaining oil in another pan, add the mushrooms and cook over a low heat, stirring occasionally, for 5–7 minutes. Add them to the stock with the beans. Stir in the reserved meat and the peppermint, heat through and serve.

Kale Soup Energy 411kcal/1740kJ; Protein 13.2g; Carbohydrate 69.3g, of which sugars 6.2g; Fat 11g, of which saturates 4.1g; Cholesterol 15mg; Calcium 140mg; Fibre 4g; Sodium 812mg.
Hare Soup Energy 297kcal/1242kJ; Protein 24g; Carbohydrate 18.7g, of which sugars 8.5g; Fat 12.9g, of which saturates 2.9g; Cholesterol 69mg; Calcium 159mg; Fibre 6.4g; Sodium 299mg.

Leek Soufflé

Some people think of a soufflé as a dinner party dish, and a rather tricky one at that. However, others frequently serve them for family meals because they are quick and easy to make. This version makes the most of tasty winter leeks.

Serves 2–3
15ml/1 tbsp sunflower oil
40g/1½oz/3 tbsp butter

2 leeks, thinly sliced
about 300ml/½ pint/
  1¼ cups milk
25g/1oz/¼ cup plain
  (all-purpose) flour
4 eggs, separated
75g/3oz Gruyère or Emmenthal
  cheese, grated
salt and ground black pepper

1 Preheat the oven to 180°C/350°F/Gas 4 and butter a large soufflé dish. Heat the sunflower oil and 15g/½oz/1 tbsp of the butter in a pan or flameproof casserole and fry the leeks over low heat for about 4–5 minutes until softened but not browned, stirring occasionally.

2 Stir in the milk and bring to the boil. Cover and simmer for 4–5 minutes until the leeks are tender. Strain the liquid through a sieve (strainer) into a measuring jug (cup).

3 Melt the remaining butter in a pan, stir in the flour and cook for 1 minute. Remove the pan from the heat. Make up the reserved liquid with milk to 300ml/½ pint/1¼ cups.

4 Gradually stir the milk into the pan to make a smooth sauce. Return to the heat and bring to the boil, stirring. When thickened, remove from the heat. Cool slightly and then beat in the egg yolks, and add the cheese and the leeks.

5 In a large, grease-free bowl, whisk the egg whites until stiff peaks form. Using a large metal spoon, fold the eggs into the leek and egg mixture.

6 Pour into the prepared soufflé dish and bake in the oven for about 30 minutes until golden and puffy. Serve immediately.

Leek and Onion Tartlets

These winter tartlets look great in individual tins.

Serves 6
25g/1oz/2 tbsp butter
1 onion, thinly sliced
2.5ml/½ tsp dried thyme
450g/1lb leeks, thinly sliced
50g/2oz Gruyère cheese, grated
3 eggs
300ml/½ pint/1¼ cups single
  (light) cream

pinch of freshly grated nutmeg
salt and ground black pepper
mixed salad leaves, to serve

For the pastry
175g/6oz/1⅓ cup plain
  (all-purpose) flour
75g/3oz/6 tbsp cold butter
1 egg yolk
30–45ml/2–3 tbsp cold water
2.5ml/½ tsp salt

1 Make the pastry. Sift the flour into a bowl and add the butter. Rub the butter into the flour until it resembles breadcrumbs. Make a well in the centre of the mixture. Beat together the egg yolk, water and salt, pour into the well and combine the flour and liquid until it begins to stick together. Form into a ball. Wrap and chill for 30 minutes.

2 Butter six 10cm/4in tartlet tins (muffin pans). Roll out the dough until 3mm/⅛in thick, then cut out rounds with a 12.5cm/5in cutter. Press the rounds into the tins. Re-roll the trimmings and line the remaining tins. Prick the bases and chill.

3 Preheat the oven to 190°C/375°F/Gas 5. Line the cases with foil and fill with baking beans. Place on a baking sheet and bake for 6–8 minutes until golden. Remove the foil and beans and bake for 2 minutes. Transfer to a wire rack to cool. Reduce the oven temperature to 180°C/350°F/Gas 4.

4 In a large pan, melt the butter. Cook the onion and thyme for 3–5 minutes, then add the leeks for 10–12 minutes. Divide the mixture among the cases and sprinkle each with cheese.

5 Beat together the eggs, cream, nutmeg and seasoning. Place the cases on a baking sheet and pour in the mixture. Bake for 15–20 minutes until golden. Cool on a wire rack slightly, then serve warm or at room temperature with salad leaves.

Leek Soufflé Energy 409kcal/1702kJ; Protein 20.6g; Carbohydrate 14.4g, of which sugars 7.3g; Fat 30.4g, of which saturates 14.8g; Cholesterol 310mg; Calcium 388mg; Fibre 2.5g; Sodium 506mg.
Leek Tartlets Energy 422kcal/1755kJ; Protein 11.5g; Carbohydrate 26.8g, of which sugars 3.9g; Fat 30.4g, of which saturates 17.7g; Cholesterol 200mg; Calcium 189mg; Fibre 2.7g; Sodium 215mg.

Gruyère and Potato Soufflés

This potato recipe can be prepared in advance, if you are entertaining, and given its second baking just before you serve it up.

Serves 4
225g/8oz floury potatoes
2 eggs, separated

175g/6oz/1½ cups Gruyère
  cheese, grated
50g/2oz/½ cup self-raising
  (self-rising) flour
50g/2oz spinach leaves
butter, for greasing
salt and ground black pepper
salad leaves, to serve

1 Preheat the oven to 200°C/400°F/Gas 6. Cook the potatoes in lightly salted boiling water for around 20 minutes until very tender. Drain the potatoes and mash thoroughly before adding the two egg yolks and mixing to combine.

2 Stir in half of the Gruyère cheese and all of the flour. Season to taste with salt and pepper.

3 Finely chop the spinach leaves and gently fold into the potato and egg yolk mixture.

4 Whip the egg whites until they form soft peaks. Fold a little of the egg white into the mixture to loosen it slightly. Using a large metal spoon, then fold the remaining egg white into the mixture.

5 Butter four large ramekin dishes. Pour the mixture in, place on a baking sheet and bake for 20 minutes. Remove from the oven and leave to cool.

6 Turn the soufflés out on to a baking sheet and sprinkle with the remaining cheese. Bake again for 5 minutes and serve immediately with salad leaves.

> **Variation**
> For a different flavouring, try replacing the Gruyère with a crumbled blue cheese, such as Stilton or Shropshire Blue cheeses, which have a more intense taste than the Gruyère.

Potato Skins with Cajun Dip

Divinely crisp, these potato skins are great on their own, or served with this piquant dip as a garnish or to the side. They are delicious as a snack, or as a tasty accompaniment to a winter feast.

Serves 2
2 large baking potatoes
vegetable oil, for deep frying

For the dip
120ml/4fl oz/½ cup natural
  (plain) yogurt
1 garlic clove, crushed
5ml/1 tsp tomato purée (paste)
2.5ml/½ tsp green chilli purée or
  ½ small green chilli, chopped
1.5ml/¼ tsp celery salt
salt and ground black pepper

1 Preheat the oven to 180°C/350°F/Gas 4. Bake the potatoes for 45–50 minutes until tender. Remove from the oven and set aside to cool slightly.

2 When the potatoes have cooled down enough to handle, cut them in half and scoop out the flesh, leaving a thin layer on the skins. Keep the flesh for another meal.

3 To make the dip, mix together all the ingredients and chill in the refrigerator until the skins are ready.

4 Heat a 1cm/½in layer of oil in a large pan or deep-fat fryer. Cut each potato half in half again, then fry them until crisp and golden on both sides.

5 Drain on kitchen paper, sprinkle with salt and black pepper and serve with a bowl of dip or a dollop of dip in each skin.

> **Cook's Tips**
> • If you prefer, you can microwave the potatoes to save time. This will take about 10 minutes.
> • The scooped-out flesh from the potatoes is delicious if mixed with leftover winter vegetables such as leeks or cabbage, then formed into small cakes and fried in a little oil until golden.

Gruyère Soufflés Energy 304kcal/1270kJ; Protein 16.7g; Carbohydrate 19g, of which sugars 1.2g; Fat 17.5g, of which saturates 10.4g; Cholesterol 138mg; Calcium 380mg; Fibre 1.2g; Sodium 376mg.
Potato Skins Energy 211kcal/873kJ; Protein 2.7g; Carbohydrate 12.5g, of which sugars 3.3g; Fat 17g, of which saturates 2.2g; Cholesterol 0mg; Calcium 62mg; Fibre 0.7g; Sodium 35mg.

Pineapple with Ginger and Chilli

This fruity seasonal salad is delicious when served alongside spicy dishes.

Serves 4

30ml/2 tbsp groundnut (peanut) oil
2 garlic cloves, finely shredded
40g/1 ½oz fresh root ginger, peeled and finely shredded
2 red Thai chillies, seeded and finely shredded
1 pineapple, trimmed, peeled, cored and cut into chunks
15ml/1 tbsp Thai fish sauce
30ml/2 tbsp soy sauce
15ml–30ml/1–2 tbsp sugar
30ml/2 tbsp roasted unsalted peanuts, finely chopped
1 lime, cut into quarters, to serve

1 Heat a large wok or heavy pan and add the oil. Stir in the garlic, ginger and chilli. Stir-fry until they begin to colour. Add the pineapple and stir-fry until the edges turn golden.

2 Stir in the fish sauce, soy sauce and sugar to taste and stir-fry until the pineapple begins to caramelize. Transfer to a serving dish, sprinkle with the peanuts and serve with lime wedges.

Beetroot with Fresh Mint

For adding a splash of colour to a cold wintry day, this salad is hard to beat. The dressing brings out the earthy flavour of beetroot.

Serves 4

4–6 cooked beetroot (beets), peeled and diced
5–10ml/1–2 tsp sugar
15–30ml/1–2 tbsp balsamic vinegar
juice of ½ lemon
30ml/2 tbsp extra virgin olive oil
1 bunch fresh mint, leaves stripped and thinly sliced
salt

1 Put the cooked beetroot in a bowl. Add the sugar, balsamic vinegar, lemon juice, olive oil and a pinch of salt and toss together.

2 Add half the thinly sliced fresh mint to the salad and toss lightly. Chill the salad for about 1 hour. Serve garnished with the remaining thinly sliced mint leaves.

Curried Red Cabbage Slaw

A variation on a classic, this spicy coleslaw is excellent for adding flavour and colour to a meal on a winter's day. Quick and easy to make, it is a useful dish for a last-minute gathering.

Serves 4–6

½ red cabbage, thinly sliced
1 red (bell) pepper, chopped or very thinly sliced
½ red onion, chopped
60ml/4 tbsp red or white wine vinegar or cider vinegar
60ml/4 tbsp sugar, or to taste
120ml/4fl oz/½ cup Greek (US strained plain) yogurt or natural (plain) yogurt
120ml/4fl oz/½ cup mayonnaise, preferably home-made
1.5ml/¼ tsp curry powder
2–3 handfuls of raisins
salt and ground black pepper

1 Put the cabbage, red pepper and red onions in a bowl and toss to combine thoroughly.

2 Heat the vinegar and sugar in a small pan until the sugar has dissolved, then pour over the vegetables. Leave to cool slightly.

3 Mix together the yogurt and mayonnaise, then stir into the cabbage mixture. Season to taste with curry powder, salt and ground black pepper, then mix in the raisins.

4 Chill the salad in the refrigerator for at least 2 hours before serving. Just before serving, drain off any excess liquid and briefly stir the slaw again.

Cook's Tip
If you have the time, it is worth making your own mayonnaise at home. If not, buy the best quality you can find.

Variation
To ring the changes, add extra ingredients to the basic slaw. Choose sliced celery, olives, raisins, chopped red (bell) pepper, chopped cooked potatoes and chopped spring onions (scallions).

Pineapple with Ginger Energy 203kcal/844kJ; Protein 2.7g; Carbohydrate 16g, of which sugars 15.4g; Fat 14.7g, of which saturates 1.9g; Cholesterol 0mg; Calcium 31mg; Fibre 1.8g; Sodium 810mg.
Beetroot with Fresh Mint Energy 90kcal/378kJ; Protein 1.7g; Carbohydrate 8.9g, of which sugars 8.3g; Fat 5.6g, of which saturates 0.8g; Cholesterol 0mg; Calcium 21mg; Fibre 1.9g; Sodium 66mg.
Red Cabbage Slaw Energy 286kcal/1194kJ; Protein 3.5g; Carbohydrate 31.6g, of which sugars 31g; Fat 17g, of which saturates 2.6g; Cholesterol 17mg; Calcium 108mg; Fibre 3.1g; Sodium 134mg.

Chicory Salad with Roquefort

The distinctive flavour and creamy richness of Roquefort cheese perfectly complements the slightly bitter taste of the salad leaves in this palate-tingling salad. Chicory, also known as Belgian endive, and celery are both in season during the winter months. Warmed crusty bread makes the ideal accompaniment.

Serves 4
30ml/2 tbsp red wine vinegar
5ml/1 tsp Dijon mustard
60ml/2fl oz/¼ cup walnut oil
15–30ml/1–2 tbsp sunflower oil
2 chicory (Belgian endive) heads, white or red
1 celery heart or 4 celery sticks, peeled and cut into julienne strips
75g/3oz/1 cup walnut halves, lightly toasted
30ml/2 tbsp chopped fresh parsley
115g/4oz Roquefort cheese, crumbled
fresh parsley sprigs, to garnish

1 Whisk together the vinegar and mustard in a small bowl, then whisk in salt and pepper to taste. Slowly whisk in the walnut oil, then the sunflower oil.

2 Divide the chicory heads into leaves and arrange decoratively on individual plates. Sprinkle over the celery julienne strips, walnut halves and chopped parsley.

3 Crumble equal amounts of Roquefort cheese over each serving and drizzle a little vinaigrette over each. Garnish with parsley sprigs and serve immediately.

Cook's Tip
Roquefort is a rich, blue cheese with a soft, crumbly texture and quite a sharp flavour. Good for salads or cooking, it is made in the village of Roquefort in France and is produced from ewe's milk. The good sheep-grazing land and limestone caves in this district contribute to giving the cheese its unique flavour. Roquefort is widely available in larger supermarkets, but if you have difficulty in finding it, you could use another well-flavoured blue cheese, such as Gorgonzola or Stilton.

Winter Coleslaw

A delicious and nutritious mixture of crunchy, seasonal vegetables, fruit and nuts, tossed together in a mayonnaise dressing.

Serves 6
225g/8oz white cabbage
1 large carrot
175g/6oz/¾ cup ready-to-eat dried apricots
50g/2oz/½ cup walnuts
50g/2oz/½ cup hazelnuts
115g/4oz/⅔ cup raisins
30ml/2 tbsp chopped fresh parsley
105ml/7 tbsp mayonnaise
75ml/5 tbsp natural (plain) yogurt
salt and ground black pepper
fresh chives, to garnish (optional)

1 Finely shred the cabbage, removing any tough core pieces, and coarsely grate the carrot. Place both in a large mixing bowl.

2 Roughly chop the dried apricots, walnuts and hazelnuts. Stir them into the cabbage and carrot mixture with the raisins and chopped parsley.

3 In a separate bowl, mix together the mayonnaise and yogurt and season to taste with salt and pepper.

4 Add the mayonnaise dressing to the cabbage mixture and toss together to mix. Cover the bowl with cling film (plastic wrap) and set aside in a cool place for at least 30 minutes before serving, to allow the flavours to mingle. Garnish with a few fresh chives and serve.

Variations
• *For a salad that is lower in fat, use low-fat natural (plain) yogurt and reduced-calorie mayonnaise.*
• *Instead of walnuts and hazelnuts, use flaked almonds and chopped pistachios.*
• *Omit the dried apricots and add a cored and chopped, unpeeled eating apple.*
• *Substitute other dried fruit or a mixture for the apricots – try nectarines, peaches or prunes.*

Winter Coleslaw Energy 309kcal/1285kJ; Protein 4.3g; Carbohydrate 19.1g, of which sugars 18.8g; Fat 24.5g, of which saturates 2.9g; Cholesterol 13mg; Calcium 72mg; Fibre 2.5g; Sodium 103mg.
Chicory Salad Energy 361kcal/1488kJ; Protein 9.4g; Carbohydrate 1.5g, of which sugars 1.3g; Fat 35.3g, of which saturates 7.9g; Cholesterol 22mg; Calcium 204mg; Fibre 1.8g; Sodium 423mg.

Stir-fried Cauliflower with Garlic Crumbs

This method of cooking cauliflower is very simple and it makes a great accompaniment to any meat or dairy meal. The garlic breadcrumbs add bite and flavour. If you are not keen on garlic it can be omitted and the cauliflower can be topped with grated cheese. Brown the cheese topping under a hot grill.

Serves 4–6
1 large cauliflower, cut into
   bitesize florets
pinch of sugar
90–120ml/6-8 tbsp olive or
   vegetable oil
130g/4½ oz/2¼ cups dry white
   or wholemeal (whole-wheat)
   breadcrumbs
3–5 garlic cloves, thinly sliced
   or chopped
salt and ground black pepper

1 Steam or boil the cauliflower in a pan of water, to which you have added the sugar and a pinch of salt, until just tender. Drain the cauliflower in a colander and leave to cool.

2 Heat 60–75ml/4–5 tbsp of the olive or vegetable oil in a pan, add the breadcrumbs and cook over medium heat, tossing and turning, until browned and crisp. Add the garlic, turn once or twice, then remove from the pan and set aside.

3 Heat the remaining oil in the pan, then add the cauliflower, mashing and breaking it up a little as it lightly browns in the oil. (Do not overcook but just cook lightly in the oil.)

4 Add the garlic breadcrumbs to the pan and cook them, stirring, until well combined and some of the cauliflower is still holding its shape. Season with salt and pepper and spoon into a heated dish. Serve hot or warm.

> **Cook's Tip**
> In Israel, where this dish is popular, it is often eaten with meat or fish wrapped in filo pastry, since the textures and flavours complement each other perfectly.

Brussels Sprouts with Bacon and Caraway Seeds

Brussels sprouts are not usually associated with stir-frying, but this style of cooking helps to retain their crunchy texture. Shredding the sprouts and cooking them briefly guarantees that there will not be a single soggy sprout in sight.

Serves 4
450g/1lb Brussels sprouts,
   trimmed and washed
30ml/2 tbsp sunflower oil
2 streaky (fatty) bacon rashers
   (strips), finely chopped
10ml/2 tsp caraway seeds,
   lightly crushed
salt and ground black pepper

1 Using a sharp knife, cut the Brussels sprouts into fine shreds and set aside. Heat the oil in a wok or large frying pan and add the bacon. Cook for 1–2 minutes, or until the bacon is beginning to turn golden.

2 Add the shredded sprouts to the wok or pan and stir-fry for 1–2 minutes, or until lightly cooked.

3 Season the sprouts with salt and ground black pepper to taste and stir in the caraway seeds. Cook for a further 30 seconds, then serve immediately.

> **Variation**
> Add a few sliced water chestnuts to the stir-fry to introduce an extra crunchy texture. Cook fresh chestnuts for about 5 minutes, canned for 2 minutes to retain their crispness.

> **Cook's Tips**
> • The sulphurous flavour that many people dislike in Brussels sprouts is produced when they are overcooked. Briefly stir-frying them avoids this problem.
> • Caraway seeds have a flavour rather like aniseed and are much used in central and eastern European cookery.

Kale with Mustard Dressing

Sea kale is used for this dish, available in many regions between January and March. Use curly kale if you can't get sea kale, although you should boil it briefly for a few minutes.

Serves 4
250g/9oz sea kale or curly kale
45ml/3 tbsp light olive oil
5ml/1 tsp wholegrain mustard
15ml/1 tbsp white wine vinegar
pinch of caster (superfine) sugar
salt and ground black pepper

1 Wash the sea kale, drain thoroughly, then trim it and cut in two. Whisk the oil into the mustard. When it is blended completely, whisk in the wine vinegar. It should begin to thicken.

2 Season the dressing to taste with sugar, salt and pepper. Toss the sea kale in the dressing and serve immediately.

Spiced Greens

Here is a really good way to enliven your winter greens, great for cabbage but also good for kale.

Serves 4
1 medium cabbage

15ml/1 tbsp groundnut
    (peanut) oil
5ml/1 tsp grated fresh root ginger
2 garlic cloves, grated
2 shallots, finely chopped
2 red chillies, seeded and sliced
salt and ground black pepper

1 Remove any tough outer leaves from the cabbage, then quarter it and remove the core. Shred the leaves.

2 Pour the groundnut oil into a large pan and as it heats stir in the ginger and garlic. Add the shallots and as the pan becomes hotter add the chillies.

3 Add the greens and toss to mix. Cover the pan and reduce the heat to create some steam. Cook, shaking the pan occasionally, for about 3 minutes. Remove the lid and increase the heat to dry off the steam, season with salt and pepper and serve immediately in a heated bowl.

Colcannon

This traditional Irish dish is especially associated with Halloween, when it is likely to be made with seasonal curly kale and would have a ring hidden in it – predicting marriage during the coming year for the person who found it. At other times during the winter green cabbage is more often used.

Serves 3–4
450g/1lb potatoes, peeled
    and boiled
450g/1lb curly kale or
    cabbage, cooked
milk, if necessary
50g/2oz/¼ cup butter, plus extra
    for serving
1 large onion, finely chopped
salt and ground black pepper

1 Mash the potatoes and spoon them into a large bowl. Chop the kale or cabbage, add it to the potatoes and mix. Stir in a little milk if the mash is too stiff, and season with salt and ground black pepper.

2 Melt a little butter in a frying pan over a medium heat and add the onion. Cook for 3–4 minutes until softened. Remove and mix well with the potato and kale or cabbage.

3 Add the remainder of the butter to the hot pan. When it is very hot, turn the potato mixture on to the pan and spread it out in an even layer.

4 Fry the potato mixture until golden brown, then cut it roughly into pieces and continue frying until these are crisp and brown.

5 Spoon the colcannon into a large serving bowl or individual bowls, and add a generous knob of butter to each. Serve immediately. As the butter melts, guests can fork it in to the cabbage mixture.

Cook's Tip
This winter dish is delicious when served as an accompaniment to pork chops or sausages for a substantial meal, or you can serve it simply with fried eggs.

Kale with Mustard Dressing Energy 99kcal/409kJ; Protein 2.1g; Carbohydrate 1.9g, of which sugars 1.9g; Fat 9.3g, of which saturates 1.3g; Cholesterol 0mg; Calcium 82mg; Fibre 2g; Sodium 27mg.
Spiced Greens Energy 77kcal/322kJ; Protein 2.6g; Carbohydrate 9.9g, of which sugars 9.4g; Fat 3.1g, of which saturates 0.5g; Cholesterol 0mg; Calcium 90mg; Fibre 3.9g; Sodium 13mg.
Colcannon Energy 1224kcal/5124kJ; Protein 21.6g; Carbohydrate 162.4g, of which sugars 54.4g; Fat 58.4g, of which saturates 35.2; Cholesterol 144mg; Calcium 416mg; Fibre 23.6g; Sodium 508mg.

Baked Leek and Potato Gratin

Potatoes baked in a creamy cheese sauce make the ultimate comfort dish for a cold winter's day, whether served as an accompaniment to pork or fish or, as here, with plenty of leeks and cheese as a main course.

Serves 4–6

900g/2lb medium potatoes, thinly sliced
2 large leeks, trimmed
200g/7oz ripe Brie cheese, sliced
450ml/^{3}/$_4$ pint/scant 2 cups single (light) cream
salt and ground black pepper

1 Preheat the oven to 180°C/350°F/Gas 4. Cook the potatoes in plenty of lightly salted, boiling water for 3 minutes, until slightly softened, then drain.

2 Cut the leeks into 1cm/^{1}/$_2$in slices and blanch them in a pan of boiling water for 1–2 minutes, until softened, then drain.

3 Place half the potatoes into a lightly greased ovenproof dish and spread them out. Cover the potatoes with about two-thirds of the leeks, then add the remaining potatoes on top.

4 Tuck the cheese and the remaining leeks in among the potatoes. Season with salt and pepper and pour the cream over.

5 Bake for 1 hour, until tender and golden. Cover with foil if the top starts to overbrown before the potatoes are tender.

Cook's Tip
When preparing leeks, separate the leaves and rinse them thoroughly under cold running water, as soil and grit often get caught between the layers.

Variation
This dish can be made with vegetable stock in place of the cream if you are concerned about calories.

Carrot Bake

Carrots and rice are surprisingly well-suited partners. The characteristic stickiness of the short grain pudding rice binds all the other ingredients together to make a satisfying and comforting winter's dish.

Serves 4
500g/1^1/$_4$lb carrots, sliced
500ml/17fl oz/generous 2 cups water

5ml/1 tsp salt
100g/3^3/$_4$oz/^{1}/$_2$ cup short grain rice
100ml/3^1/$_2$fl oz/scant ^{1}/$_2$ cup milk
25g/1oz/2 tbsp butter, softened, for greasing
30ml/2 tbsp demerara (raw) sugar
2 eggs, beaten
2.5ml/^{1}/$_2$ tsp ground white pepper
25g/1oz/^{1}/$_2$ cup fine fresh breadcrumbs

1 Put the carrots in a large pan and cover generously with water. Bring the water to the boil, lower the heat and simmer for about 20 minutes until the carrots are tender. Remove the carrots with a slotted spoon and mash in a clean pan.

2 Bring the liquid the carrots were cooked in to the boil, then add the salt and the rice and simmer for 25 minutes. Add the milk and simmer until it has been absorbed.

3 Preheat the oven to 200°C/400°F/Gas 6. Use the butter to grease a deep, ovenproof dish. Transfer the cooked rice to a bowl. Add the mashed carrots, sugar and eggs and mix together. Season the mixture with salt and the ground white pepper.

4 Spoon the carrot mixture into the prepared dish and sprinkle the breadcrumbs over the top. Place in the preheated oven and bake for about 40 minutes or until golden brown. Serve immediately.

Cook's Tip
Cooking rice for a savoury dish in water first helps to speed up the cooking time. Milk can then be added halfway through to give a creamier texture to the finished dish.

Baked Leek Gratin Energy 383kcal/1597kJ; Protein 13.1g; Carbohydrate 28.2g, of which sugars 5.4g; Fat 24.2g, of which saturates 15.4g; Cholesterol 72mg; Calcium 181mg; Fibre 3.3g; Sodium 225mg.
Carrot Bake Energy 280kcal/1171kJ; Protein 7.4g; Carbohydrate 43.7g, of which sugars 18.5g; Fat 9g, of which saturates 4.4g; Cholesterol 110mg; Calcium 94mg; Fibre 3.2g; Sodium 654mg.

Carrot and Parsnip Purée

This purée features two of the favourite winter vegetables. The creaminess of purées appeals to all ages, and they are ideal partners for crisp, seasonal vegetables such as lightly cooked Savoy cabbage or pan-fried kale. If serving the purée directly on to plates, mould it by using two spoons.

Serves 6–8
350g/12oz carrots
450g/1lb parsnips
a pinch of freshly grated nutmeg
 or ground mace
15g/½oz/1 tbsp butter
about 15ml/1 tbsp single (light)
 cream or crème fraîche
a small bunch of parsley,
 chopped, plus extra to garnish
salt and ground black pepper

1 Peel the carrots and slice fairly thinly. Peel the parsnips and cut into bitesize chunks.

2 Boil the carrots and parsnips in separate pans of lightly salted water until tender. Drain them well, then purée them together in a food processor, with the grated nutmeg or mace, a generous seasoning of salt and ground black pepper, and the butter. Whizz until smooth.

3 Transfer the purée to a mixing bowl and beat in the single cream or crème fraîche. Add the fresh parsley for extra flavour.

4 Transfer the carrot and parsnip purée to a warmed serving bowl, sprinkle with the remaining parsley to garnish, and serve immediately, as vegetable purées tend to lose their heat rapidly.

Cook's Tips
Any leftover purée can be thinned to taste with good-quality chicken or vegetable stock and heated to make a quick home-made soup. Add more seasoning if needed.

Variation
Use diced sweet potato instead of the carrots.

Parsnip and Chickpea Stew

Sweet parsnips go very well with the spices in this Indian-style winter stew, made in the slow cooker.

Serves 4
5 garlic cloves, finely chopped
1 small onion, chopped
5cm/2in piece fresh root ginger,
 finely chopped
2 green chillies, seeded and chopped
75ml/5 tbsp cold water
60ml/4 tbsp groundnut (peanut) oil
5ml/1 tsp cumin seeds
10ml/2 tsp coriander seeds
5ml/1 tsp ground turmeric
2.5ml/½ tsp chilli powder
 or mild paprika
50g/2oz/½ cup cashew nuts,
 toasted and ground
225g/8oz tomatoes, peeled
 and chopped
400g/14oz can chickpeas, drained
 and rinsed
900g/2lb parsnips, cut into chunks
350ml/12fl oz/1½ cups boiling
 vegetable stock
juice of 1 lime, to taste
salt and ground black pepper
chopped fresh coriander (cilantro)
 leaves, toasted cashew nuts and
 natural (plain) yogurt, to serve

1 Reserve 10ml/2 tsp of the garlic, then place the remainder in a food processor or blender with the onion, ginger and half the chillies. Add the water and process to a smooth paste.

2 Heat the oil in a large frying pan, add the cumin seeds and cook for 30 seconds. Stir in the coriander seeds, turmeric, chilli powder or paprika and the ground cashew nuts. Add the ginger and chilli paste and cook, stirring frequently, until the paste starts to bubble and the water begins to evaporate.

3 Add the tomatoes to the pan and cook for 1 minute. Transfer the mixture to the ceramic cooking pot and switch the slow cooker to high. Add the chickpeas and parsnips to the pot and stir to coat in the spicy tomato mixture, then stir in the stock and season with salt and pepper. Cover with the lid and cook on high for 4 hours, or until the parsnips are tender.

4 Stir half the lime juice, the reserved garlic and green chillies into the stew. Re-cover and cook for 30 minutes more, then taste and add more lime juice if needed. Spoon on to plates and sprinkle with fresh coriander leaves and toasted cashew nuts. Serve immediately, with a generous spoonful of natural yogurt.

Carrot and Parsnip Purée Energy 71kcal/298kJ; Protein 1.5g; Carbohydrate 10.7g, of which sugars 6.6g; Fat 2.7g, of which saturates 1.4g; Cholesterol 5mg; Calcium 49mg; Fibre 4g; Sodium 31mg.
Parsnip Stew Energy 453kcal/1899kJ; Protein 14.8g; Carbohydrate 50.1g, of which sugars 16.6g; Fat 23g, of which saturates 4.3g; Cholesterol 0mg; Calcium 148mg; Fibre 15.8g; Sodium 394mg.

Halibut with Leek and Ginger

Generally fish needs to be absolutely fresh, but halibut needs to mature for a day or two to bring out the flavour. Sometimes the catch is so fresh the fish needs to be refrigerated for a day or so before cooking.

Serves 4
2 leeks
50g/2oz piece fresh root ginger
4 halibut steaks, approximately
175g/6oz each (see Cook's Tip)
15ml/1 tbsp olive oil
75g/3oz/6 tbsp butter
salt and ground black pepper
mashed potato, to serve

1 Trim the leeks, discarding the coarse outer leaves, the very dark green tops and the root end. Cut them into 5cm/2in lengths, then slice into thin matchsticks. Wash thoroughly.

2 Peel the fresh ginger as best you can, then slice it very thinly and cut the slices into thin sticks.

3 Dry the halibut on kitchen paper. Heat a large pan with the oil and add 50g/2oz/¼ cup of the butter. As it begins to bubble, place the steaks carefully in the pan, skin side down. Allow the halibut to colour – about 3–4 minutes. Then turn the steaks over, reduce the heat and cook for about a further 10 minutes.

4 Remove the fish from the pan, set aside and keep warm. Add the leeks and ginger to the pan, stir to mix, then allow the leeks to soften (they may colour slightly but this is fine). Once softened, season with a little salt and ground black pepper. Cut the remaining butter into small pieces then, off the heat, gradually stir into the pan.

5 Serve the halibut steaks topped with the leek and ginger mixture. Accompany with mashed potato, if you like.

Cook's Tip
Ask your fishmonger for flattish halibut steaks that are not too thick as you want to cook them in a pan on the stove and not in the oven. Also ask him or her to skin them for you.

Fillets of Turbot with Oysters

This luxurious dish is perfect in winter as the main ingredients are at their best.

Serves 4
12 Pacific (rock) oysters
115g/4oz/½ cup butter
2 carrots, cut into julienne strips
200g/7oz celeriac, cut into
julienne strips
the white parts of 2 leeks, cut
into julienne strips
375ml/13fl oz/generous 1½ cups
Champagne or dry white
sparkling wine (about ½ bottle)
105ml/7 tbsp whipping cream
1 turbot, about 1.75kg/4–4½lb,
filleted and skinned
salt and ground white pepper

1 Using an oyster knife, open the oysters over a bowl to catch the juices, then carefully remove them, discarding the shells, and place them in a separate bowl. Set aside until required.

2 Melt 25g/1oz/2 tbsp of the butter in a shallow pan, add the vegetable julienne and cook over a low heat until tender but not coloured. Pour in half the Champagne or sparkling wine and cook very gently until all the liquid has evaporated. Keep the heat low so that the vegetables do not colour.

3 Strain the oyster juices into a small pan and add the cream and the remaining Champagne or wine. Simmer until the mixture has reduced a little. Dice half the remaining butter and whisk it into the sauce until smooth. Season to taste, then pour the sauce into a blender and process until velvety smooth.

4 Return the sauce to the pan, bring it to just below boiling point, then drop in the oysters. Poach for 1 minute, to warm but barely cook. Keep warm, but do not let the sauce boil.

5 Season the turbot fillets. Heat the remaining butter in a large frying pan, then cook the fillets over medium heat for about 2–3 minutes on each side, until cooked through and golden.

6 Cut each turbot fillet into three pieces and arrange on individual warmed plates. Pile the vegetable julienne on top, place three oysters around the turbot fillets on each plate and pour the sauce around the edge.

Halibut with Leek Energy 364kcal/1520kJ; Protein 39.1g; Carbohydrate 2.7g, of which sugars 2.1g; Fat 21.9g, of which saturates 10.8g; Cholesterol 101mg; Calcium 75mg; Fibre 1.9g; Sodium 221mg.
Fillets of Turbot Energy 752kcal/3125kJ; Protein 66.7g; Carbohydrate 9.2g, of which sugars 8g; Fat 44.1g, of which saturates 23.9g; Cholesterol 106mg; Calcium 252mg; Fibre 1.4g; Sodium 370mg.

Smoked Haddock Bake with a Cheese Crumb

Haddock is available throughout winter and is a very popular and versatile fish. It takes to smoking very well and this is a way of enjoying the fish, even when it isn't in season. Serve this comforting dish as a filling appetizer, or accompany it with crusty bread and a leafy winter salad as a light meal or snack.

Serves 4
350g/12oz smoked haddock
450ml/¾ pint/scant 2 cups milk
25g/1oz/2 tbsp butter
25g/1oz/4 tbsp plain
   (all-purpose) flour
115g/4oz mature (sharp)
   Cheddar cheese, grated
60ml/4 tbsp fresh breadcrumbs
salt and ground black pepper
crusty bread and a leafy salad,
   to serve

1 Remove and discard all skin and bones from the haddock and cut the fish into strips.

2 Put the milk, butter and flour into a pan and season with salt and black pepper. Over medium heat and whisking constantly, bring to the boil and bubble gently for 2–3 minutes until thick and smooth.

3 Add the haddock and half the cheese to the hot sauce and bring it just back to the boil to melt the cheese.

4 Divide the mixture between individual flameproof dishes or ramekins. Toss together the remaining cheese and the breadcrumbs and sprinkle the mixture over the top of each filled dish.

5 Put the dishes under a hot grill (broiler) until bubbling and golden. Serve immediately with crusty bread.

> **Cook's Tip**
> *The flavour and colour of this dish is best when made with pale, undyed smoked haddock rather than the bright yellow artificially dyed variety.*

Smoked Haddock with Mustard Cabbage

This seasonal dish is very simple and quick to make and yet tastes absolutely delicious. Serve with baked potatoes for a main meal.

Serves 4
1 Savoy or pointu cabbage
675g/1½lb undyed smoked
   haddock fillet
300ml/½ pint/1¼ cups milk
½ onion, sliced into rings
2 bay leaves
½ lemon, sliced
4 white peppercorns
4 ripe tomatoes
50g/2oz/¼ cup butter
30ml/2 tbsp wholegrain mustard
juice of 1 lemon
salt and ground black pepper
30ml/2 tbsp chopped fresh
   parsley, to garnish

1 Cut the cabbage in half, remove the central core and thick ribs, then shred the cabbage. Cook in a pan of lightly salted, boiling water, or steam over boiling water for about 10 minutes, until just tender. Leave in the pan or steamer until required.

2 Meanwhile, put the haddock in a large shallow pan with the milk, onion and bay leaves. Add the lemon slices and peppercorns. Bring to simmering point, cover and poach until the fish flakes easily when tested with the tip of a sharp knife. Depending on the thickness of the fish, this takes 8–10 minutes. Remove the pan from the heat. Preheat the grill (broiler).

3 Cut the tomatoes in half horizontally, season them with salt and pepper and grill (broil) until lightly browned. Drain the cabbage, refresh under cold water and drain again.

4 Melt the butter in a shallow pan or wok, add the shredded cabbage and toss over the heat for 2 minutes. Mix in the mustard and season to taste, then tip the cabbage into a warmed serving dish.

5 Drain the haddock. Skin and cut the fish into four pieces. Place on top of the cabbage with some onion rings and grilled (broiled) tomato halves. Pour on the lemon juice, then sprinkle with chopped parsley and serve.

Haddock Bake Energy 363kcal/1525kJ; Protein 30.1g; Carbohydrate 21.8g, of which sugars 5.8g; Fat 17.4g, of which saturates 10.8g; Cholesterol 79mg; Calcium 396mg; Fibre 0.5g; Sodium 1073mg.
Smoked Haddock Energy 319kcal/1340kJ; Protein 36.1g; Carbohydrate 14.2g, of which sugars 13.7g; Fat 13.1g, of which saturates 7.3g; Cholesterol 90mg; Calcium 146mg; Fibre 4.2g; Sodium 1512mg.

Haddock with Spicy Puy Lentils

Grey-green Puy lentils have a delicate taste and texture and hold their shape during cooking, which makes them particularly good for slow cooker dishes. Haddock is a highly welcome addition to the winter kitchen.

Serves 4
175g/6oz/³⁄₄ cup Puy lentils
600ml/1 pint/2¹⁄₂ cups near-
    boiling vegetable stock

30ml/2 tbsp olive oil
1 onion, finely chopped
2 celery sticks, finely chopped
1 red chilli, halved, seeded
    and finely chopped
2.5ml/¹⁄₂ tsp ground cumin
four thick 150g/5oz pieces of
    haddock fillet or steak
10ml/2 tsp lemon juice
25g/1oz/2 tbsp butter, softened
5ml/1 tsp finely grated lemon rind
salt and ground black pepper
lemon wedges, to garnish

1 Put the lentils in a sieve (strainer) and rinse under cold running water. Drain well, then tip into the ceramic cooking pot. Pour over the hot vegetable stock, cover with the lid and switch the slow cooker on to high.

2 Heat the oil in a frying pan, add the onion and cook gently for 8 minutes. Stir in the celery, chilli and cumin, and cook for a further 2 minutes, or until soft but not coloured. Add the mixture to the lentils, stir, re-cover and cook for about 2¹⁄₂ hours.

3 Meanwhile, rinse the haddock pieces and pat dry on kitchen paper. Sprinkle them with the lemon juice. In a clean bowl, beat together the butter, lemon rind, salt and ground black pepper.

4 Put the haddock on top of the lentils, then dot the lemon butter over the top. Cover and cook for 45 minutes–1 hour, or until the fish flakes easily, the lentils are tender and most of the stock has been absorbed. Serve immediately, garnished with the lemon wedges.

Cook's Tip
Any firm white fish can be cooked in this way. Both cod and swordfish give particularly good results.

Kedgeree

A popular Victorian breakfast dish, kedgeree has its origins in kitchiri, an Indian dish of rice and lentils. It can be flavoured with curry powder, but this recipe is mild.

Serves 4
500g/1¹⁄₄lb smoked haddock
115g/4oz/generous ¹⁄₂ cup
    basmati rice

50g/2oz/4 tbsp butter, diced, plus
    extra for greasing
30ml/2 tbsp lemon juice
150ml/¹⁄₄ pint/²⁄₃ cup single
    (light) cream or sour cream
pinch of freshly grated nutmeg
pinch of cayenne pepper
2 hard-boiled eggs, peeled and cut
    into wedges
30ml/2 tbsp chopped
    fresh parsley
salt and ground black pepper

1 Put the haddock in a shallow pan, pour in just enough water to cover and heat to simmering point. Poach the fish for about 10 minutes, until the flesh flakes easily when tested with the tip of a sharp knife. Lift the fish out of the liquid, then remove any skin and bones and flake the flesh. Reserve the cooking liquid.

2 Pour the cooking liquid into a measuring jug (cup) and make up the volume with water to 250ml/8fl oz/1 cup.

3 Pour the measured liquid into a pan and bring it to the boil. Add the rice, stir, then lower the heat, cover and simmer for about 10 minutes, until the rice is tender and the liquid has been absorbed. Meanwhile, preheat the oven to 180°C/350°F/ Gas 4 and butter a baking dish.

4 When the rice is cooked, remove it from the heat and stir in the lemon juice, cream, flaked haddock, grated nutmeg and cayenne pepper. Add the egg wedges to the rice mixture and stir in gently.

5 Transfer the rice mixture into the prepared baking dish. Level the surface and dot with butter. Cover the dish loosely with foil and bake for about 25 minutes.

6 Stir the chopped parsley into the baked kedgeree and add seasoning to taste. Serve immediately.

Haddock with Lentils Energy 366kcal/1538kJ; Protein 38.9g; Carbohydrate 25.2g, of which sugars 3.2g; Fat 12.8g, of which saturates 4.3g; Cholesterol 82mg; Calcium 64mg; Fibre 4.7g; Sodium 353mg.
Kedgeree Energy 320kcal/1336kJ; Protein 15.6g; Carbohydrate 46.6g, of which sugars 0g; Fat 7.6g, of which saturates 3.3g; Cholesterol 149mg; Calcium 39mg; Fibre 0g; Sodium 357mg.

Sea Bass with Orange Chilli Salsa

The chilli citrus salsa has a freshness which provides the perfect contrast to the wonderful flavour of fresh sea bass.

Serves 4
4 sea bass fillets
salt and ground black pepper

fresh coriander (cilantro),
  to garnish

For the salsa
2 fresh green chillies
2 oranges or pink grapefruit
1 small onion

1 Make the salsa. Roast the chillies in a dry griddle pan until the skins are blistered, being careful not to let the flesh burn. Put them in a strong plastic bag and tie the top to keep the steam in. Set aside for 20 minutes.

2 Slice the top and bottom off each orange or grapefruit then cut off all the peel and pith. Cut between the membranes and put each segment in a bowl.

3 Remove the chillies from the bag and peel off the skins. Cut off the stalks, then slit the chillies and scrape out the seeds. Chop the flesh finely. Cut the onion in half and slice it thinly. Add the onion and chillies to the orange pieces and mix lightly. Season and chill.

4 Season the sea bass fillets. Line a steamer with baking parchment, allowing extra to hang over the sides to help lift out the fish after cooking. Place the empty steamer over a pan of water and bring to the boil.

5 Place the fish in a single layer in the steamer. Cover and steam for 8 minutes, or until just cooked. Garnish with coriander and serve with the salsa and some seasonal vegetables.

> **Cook's Tip**
> If the fish has not been scaled, do this by running the back of a small filleting knife against the grain of the scales.

Sea Bass in a Salt Crust

Baking fish in a crust of sea salt keeps in the flavours, enhancing the natural taste of the fish. It is a popular way of cooking fish on the Greek islands, where large outside ovens are used to prevent the inside of buildings becoming too hot. Any firm fish can be cooked with a salt crust, but it is well suited to the seasonal sea bass.

Serves 4
1 sea bass, about 1kg/2¼lb, cleaned and scaled
1 sprig fresh fennel
1 sprig fresh rosemary
1 sprig fresh thyme
2kg/4½lb coarse sea salt
mixed peppercorns
seaweed or samphire, blanched, to garnish
salt and ground black pepper
lemon slices, to serve

1 Preheat the oven to 240°C/475°F/Gas 9. Spread half the salt on a shallow baking tray (ideally oval or rectangular).

2 Wash out the sea bass and dry any excess moisture with kitchen paper. Open the fish and lightly season the insides with salt and freshly ground black pepper, then fill the cavity of the fish with all the fresh herbs. Do not worry if the fish does not close properly as the herbs will become much more compact as soon as they have been heated through and cooked.

3 Lay the sea bass on the salt. Cover the fish with a 1cm/½in layer of salt, pressing it down firmly. Moisten the salt lightly by spraying with water from an atomizer. Bake the fish in the hot oven for 30–40 minutes, or until the salt crust is just beginning to colour.

4 Garnish the dish with seaweed or samphire and use a sharp knife to break open the salt crust at the table. Serve with lemon slices.

> **Cook's Tip**
> Make sure that you leave enough time for the oven to heat up properly, as a cooler oven will not be able to set the salt crust.

Sea Bass in a Salt Crust Energy 83kcal/351kJ; Protein 16.1g; Carbohydrate 0g, of which sugars 0g; Fat 2.1g, of which saturates 0.3g; Cholesterol 67mg; Calcium 109mg; Fibre 0g; Sodium 2021mg.
Sea Bass with Orange Energy 181kcal/763kJ; Protein 30.2g; Carbohydrate 6.6g, of which sugars 6.3g; Fat 3.9g, of which saturates 0.6g; Cholesterol 120mg; Calcium 232mg; Fibre 1.3g; Sodium 108mg.

Chicken with Potato Dumplings

Slowly poaching chicken pieces in a creamy sauce, topped with light herb and potato dumplings, makes a delicate yet warming meal for a winter's day.

Serves 6

1 onion, chopped
300ml/½ pint/1¼ cups
  vegetable stock
120ml/4fl oz/½ cup white wine
4 large chicken breast fillets
300ml/½ pint/1¼ cups single
  (light) cream

15ml/1 tbsp chopped
  fresh tarragon
salt and ground black pepper

For the dumplings

225g/8oz maincrop potatoes,
  boiled and mashed
175g/6oz/1¼ cups suet
  (US chilled, grated shortening)
115g/4oz/1 cup self-raising
  (self-rising) flour
50ml/2fl oz/¼ cup water
30ml/2 tbsp chopped mixed
  fresh herbs
salt and ground black pepper

1 Place the onion, stock and wine in a deep-sided frying pan. Add the chicken and simmer, covered, for 20 minutes.

2 Remove the chicken from the stock, cut it into chunks and set aside. Strain the stock and discard the onion. Return the stock to the pan and boil until reduced by one-third. Stir in the single cream and tarragon and simmer until just thickened. Stir in the chicken and season with salt and ground black pepper.

3 Spoon the mixture into a 900ml/1½ pint/3¾ cup ovenproof dish. Preheat the oven to 190°C/375°F/Gas 5.

4 Mix together the dumpling ingredients to make a soft dough. Divide into six and shape into balls with floured hands.

5 Place the dumplings on top of the chicken mixture and bake uncovered for 30 minutes until cooked. Serve immediately.

Cook's Tip
Make sure that you do not reduce the sauce too much before cooking in the oven as the dumplings absorb quite a lot of liquid.

Chicken with Winter Vegetables

A slow-baked winter casserole of wonderfully tender chicken, seasonal root vegetables and green lentils, finished with crème fraîche, wholegrain mustard and tarragon.

Serves 4

350g/12oz onions
350g/12oz leeks
225g/8oz carrots
450g/1lb swede (rutabaga)
30ml/2 tbsp oil
4 chicken portions, about
  900g/2lb total weight

115g/4oz/½ cup green lentils
475ml/16fl oz/2 cups
  chicken stock
300ml/½ pint/1¼ cups
  apple juice
10ml/2 tsp cornflour (cornstarch)
45ml/3 tbsp crème fraîche
10ml/2 tsp wholegrain mustard
30ml/2 tbsp chopped
  fresh tarragon
salt and ground black pepper
a few fresh tarragon sprigs,
  to garnish

1 Preheat the oven to 190°C/375°F/Gas 5. Roughly chop the onions, leeks, carrots and swede into even pieces.

2 Heat the oil in a large, flameproof casserole. Season the chicken portions with salt and pepper, and fry them until golden. Drain on kitchen paper.

3 Add the onions to the casserole and cook for 5 minutes, stirring, until they begin to soften and colour. Add the leeks, carrots, swede and lentils, and cook, stirring, over medium heat for about 2 minutes.

4 Return the chicken portions to the casserole. Pour in the stock and apple juice, and season with salt and pepper. Bring to the boil and cover with a tight-fitting lid. Cook in the oven for 50 minutes to 1 hour or until the chicken portions are tender.

5 Place the casserole over medium heat. Blend the cornflour with 30ml/2 tbsp water and add to the casserole with the crème fraîche, mustard and tarragon. Adjust the seasoning. Simmer gently for about 2 minutes, stirring. Serve immediately, garnished with tarragon sprigs.

Chicken with Dumplings Energy 552kcal/2300kJ; Protein 28.2g; Carbohydrate 26.5g, of which sugars 2.6g; Fat 37.4g, of which saturates 21g; Cholesterol 121mg; Calcium 83mg; Fibre 1.3g; Sodium 80mg.
Chicken Energy 505kcal/2132kJ; Protein 65.2g; Carbohydrate 43.8g, of which sugars 24.7g; Fat 8.9g, of which saturates 3.9g; Cholesterol 170mg; Calcium 181mg; Fibre 9.7g; Sodium 182mg.

Braised Chicken with Mashed Swede

This traditional way of cooking chicken maintains maximum flavour and produces delicious juices in the dish. It is served with a mixture of mashed swede and potato, which absorb the butter to give a delectable creamy purée.

Serves 4
75g/3oz/6 tbsp butter
15ml/1tbsp oil

1 small bunch fresh parsley
1.6kg/3¹/₂lb chicken
salt and ground black pepper

For the mashed swede
450g/1lb swede (rutabaga), cut
  into cubes
675g/1¹/₂lb potatoes, cut
  into cubes
about 115g/4oz/¹/₂ cup butter
pinch of ground allspice

1 Put half of the butter, parsley, salt and pepper inside the chicken. Heat the oil and the rest of the butter in a flameproof casserole. Add the chicken and brown on all sides. Season the outside of the chicken with salt and pepper.

2 Lower the heat, cover the pan and simmer gently for about 1 hour. Test that the chicken is cooked by inserting the point of a sharp knife into the thickest part of the thigh near the body – the juices that run out should be clear.

3 Prepare the mashed swede. Put the swede in a large pan, cover with water and season with salt. Bring to the boil, lower the heat and simmer for 15 minutes.

4 Add the potatoes to the pan of swede and simmer for 15 minutes. Drain, reserving a little water and return the vegetables to the pan. Mash well, then add the butter and allspice. Season the mashed vegetables with salt and ground black pepper.

5 When cooked, transfer the chicken to a warmed serving dish. Add a little water to the pan to make a simple gravy, stirring to deglaze the pan and scraping up any sediment from the bottom. Serve the chicken immediately with the gravy and mashed swede.

Braised Quail with Winter Vegetables

Roasting and braising are the two classic techniques for cooking quail. Here, they are cooked and served in a red wine sauce, then elegantly displayed on crisp croûtes.

Serves 4
4 quail, cleaned
175g/6oz small carrots, scrubbed
175g/6oz baby turnips
60ml/4 tbsp olive oil

4 shallots, halved
450ml/³/₄ pint/scant 2 cups
  red wine
30ml/2 tbsp Spanish brandy
salt and ground black pepper
fresh flat leaf parsley, to garnish

For the croûtes
4 slices stale bread,
  crusts removed
60ml/4 tbsp olive oil

1 Preheat the oven to 220°C/425°F/Gas 7. Season the quail with salt and ground black pepper. Using a sharp knife, cut the carrots and baby turnips into chunks. (If the carrots are very small, you can leave them whole if you prefer.)

2 Heat half the oil in a flameproof casserole and add the quail. Fry until evenly browned all over. Remove from the casserole and set aside.

3 Add more olive oil to the casserole with all the vegetables and shallots. Cook until just colouring. Return the quail to the casserole, breast sides down, and pour in the red wine. Cover and cook in the oven for 30 minutes, or until the quail are tender.

4 Meanwhile, make the croûtes. Using a 10cm/4in plain cutter stamp out rounds from the bread. Heat the oil in a frying pan and cook the bread over a high heat until golden on both sides. Drain on kitchen paper and keep warm.

5 Place the croûtes on warm plates and set a quail on top of each. Arrange the vegetables around the quail, and keep hot.

6 Boil the cooking juices hard until reduced to a syrupy consistency. Add the brandy and warm through, then season to taste. Drizzle the sauce over the quail and garnish with parsley, then serve immediately.

Braised Chicken Energy 821kcal/3410kJ; Protein 43.5g; Carbohydrate 33g, of which sugars 7.9g; Fat 58g, of which saturates 24.9g; Cholesterol 269mg; Calcium 91mg; Fibre 3.8g; Sodium 372mg.
Braised Quail Energy 591kcal/2456kJ; Protein 24.4g; Carbohydrate 14.3g, of which sugars 6.7g; Fat 38.8g, of which saturates 7.6g; Cholesterol 116mg; Calcium 68mg; Fibre 2.5g; Sodium 184mg.

Braised Partridge with Cabbage

For this seasonal dish, partridges are layered with Savoy cabbage and cooked in stock and beer.

Serves 4

2 mature partridges, cleaned and
  ready to cook
115g/4oz/1/2 cup butter
1 large Savoy cabbage, sliced
200g/7oz rindless smoked streaky
  (fatty) bacon
4 small pork sausages
4 small smoked sausages
pinch of freshly grated nutmeg
250ml/8fl oz/1 cup chicken stock
750ml/1 1/4 pints/3 cups dark
  Abbey beer or more hot
  chicken stock
2 bay leaves
4 juniper berries
salt and ground black pepper
mashed potatoes, to serve

1 Cut each partridge in half down the centre. Season with salt and pepper. Melt the butter in a large heavy frying pan. Add the partridge halves and brown them on both sides. Cover the pan with foil or a lid and cook over low heat for 30 minutes.

2 Meanwhile, bring a large pan of water to the boil. Stir in 15ml/1 tbsp salt. Add the cabbage and blanch it for 3 minutes, then drain and pat dry with kitchen paper.

3 Put the browned birds on a plate. Set aside. Reheat the fat in the pan and add the bacon and sausages. Fry for 6–8 minutes, until the bacon is crisp and the sausages are cooked.

4 Preheat the oven to 160°C/325°F/Gas 3. Grease a large baking dish (the partridges should be in a single layer). Spread half the cabbage on the base and season with salt, pepper and nutmeg. Place the partridges on top and arrange the bacon and sausages in between. Cover with the remaining cabbage and season again.

5 Pour over the hot chicken stock and beer (or both quantities of stock). Add the bay leaves and juniper berries, cover the dish and bake in the oven for 1 hour.

6 Adjust the seasoning. Mound the cabbage on a heated platter and arrange the partridges on top, with the bacon and sausages around the side. Serve with the potatoes.

Stuffed Roast Turkey

In this simple recipe, the popular winter turkey is stuffed with a rich herb stuffing and served with seasonal cranberry jelly.

Serves 6

1 turkey, about 4.5–5.5kg/10–12lb,
  washed and patted dry with
  kitchen paper
25g/1oz/2 tbsp butter, melted
salt and ground black pepper
cranberry jelly, to serve

For the stuffing
200g/7oz/3 1/2 cups fresh
  white breadcrumbs
175ml/6fl oz/3/4 cup milk
25g/1oz/2 tbsp butter
1 egg, separated
1 calf's liver, about 600g/1lb 6oz,
  finely chopped
2 onions, finely chopped
90ml/6 tbsp chopped fresh dill
10ml/2 tsp clear honey
salt and ground black pepper

1 Make the stuffing. Soak the breadcrumbs in milk until swollen. Melt the butter in a frying pan and mix 5ml/1 tsp with the egg. Heat the remaining butter and fry the liver and onions for 5 minutes, until the onions are golden brown. Set aside to cool.

2 Preheat the oven to 180°C/350°F/Gas 4. Add the cooled liver mixture to the soaked breadcrumbs then add the butter and egg yolk mixture, with the dill, honey and seasoning. Whisk the egg white to soft peaks, then fold into the mixture, stirring gently to combine thoroughly.

3 Season the turkey inside and out. Stuff the cavity with the stuffing mixture, then weigh to calculate the cooking time. Allow 20 minutes per 500g/1 1/4lb, plus an additional 20 minutes. Tuck the legs inside the cavity and tie the end shut with string. Brush over the outside with butter and transfer to a roasting pan. Place in the oven and roast for the calculated time.

4 Baste the turkey regularly, and cover with foil for the final 30 minutes if the skin gets too brown. To test it is cooked, pierce the thick part of the thigh with a knife; the juices should run clear.

5 Remove the turkey from the oven, cover with foil and leave to rest for about 15 minutes. Carve into thin slices, then spoon over the juices and serve with the stuffing and cranberry jelly.

Braised Partridge Energy 1016kcal/4227kJ; Protein 79.7g; Carbohydrate 15.2g, of which sugars 10g; Fat 66.2g, of which saturates 29g; Cholesterol 139mg; Calcium 219mg; Fibre 2.9g; Sodium 1633mg.
Stuffed Turkey Energy 740kcal/3126kJ; Protein 112.3g; Carbohydrate 35.9g, of which sugars 7.3g; Fat 13.5g, of which saturates 6.6g; Cholesterol 507mg; Calcium 122mg; Fibre 1.7g; Sodium 517mg.

Turkey Croquettes

A crisp patty of smoked turkey mixed with mashed potato and spring onions and rolled in breadcrumbs.

Serves 4

450g/1lb potatoes, diced
3 eggs
30ml/2 tbsp milk
175g/6oz smoked turkey rashers (strips), finely chopped
2 spring onions (scallions), finely sliced

115g/4oz/2 cups fresh white breadcrumbs
vegetable oil, for deep fat frying
salt and ground black pepper

For the sauce

15ml/1 tbsp olive oil
1 onion, finely chopped
400g/14oz can tomatoes, drained
30ml/2 tbsp tomato purée (paste)
15ml/1 tbsp chopped fresh parsley

1 Boil the potatoes for 20 minutes or until tender. Drain and return the pan to low heat to evaporate the excess water.

2 Mash the potatoes with two eggs and the milk. Season well with salt and black pepper. Stir in the turkey and spring onions. Chill for 1 hour.

3 Meanwhile, to make the sauce, heat the oil in a frying pan and fry the onion for 5 minutes until soft. Add the tomatoes and purée, stir and simmer for 10 minutes. Stir in the parsley, season with salt and pepper and keep warm.

4 Remove the potato mixture from the refrigerator and divide into eight pieces. Shape each piece into a sausage shape and dip in the remaining beaten egg and then the breadcrumbs.

5 Heat the oil in a pan or deep-fat fryer to 175°C/330°F and deep fry the croquettes for 5 minutes, or until golden and crisp. Serve with the sauce.

> **Cook's Tip**
> Test the oil temperature by dropping a cube of bread into it. If it sinks, rises and sizzles in 10 seconds the oil is ready to use.

Turkey Patties

Minced turkey makes deliciously light patties, which are ideal for winter meals. The recipe is a flavourful variation on a classic burger and they can also be made using minced lamb, pork or beef.

1 small red onion, finely chopped
grated rind and juice of 1 lime
small handful of fresh thyme leaves
15–30ml/1–2 tbsp olive oil
salt and ground black pepper

Serves 6

675g/1½lb minced (ground) turkey

1 Mix together the turkey, onion, lime rind and juice, thyme and seasoning. Cover and chill for up to 4 hours to allow the flavours to mingle.

2 Divide the turkey mixture into six equal portions. Shape into round patties with lightly floured hands.

3 Preheat a griddle pan. Brush the patties with oil, then place them on the pan and cook on one side for 10–12 minutes. Turn the patties over with a metal spatula, brush with more oil and cook for a further 10–12 minutes on the second side, or until cooked through. Serve immediately.

> **Cook's Tip**
> Serve the patties in split and toasted buns or pieces of crusty bread, with chutney, salad leaves and chunky fries.

> **Variations**
> • Minced (ground) chicken or minced pork could be used instead of turkey in these burgers.
> • You could also try chopped oregano, parsley or basil in place of the thyme, and lemon rind instead of lime.

Turkey Croquettes Energy 404kcal/1698kJ; Protein 19.4g; Carbohydrate 47g, of which sugars 7.7g; Fat 16.7g, of which saturates 2.4g; Cholesterol 73mg; Calcium 93mg; Fibre 3.3g; Sodium 315mg.
Turkey Patties Energy 141kcal/596kJ; Protein 24.8g; Carbohydrate 0.8g, of which sugars 0.60g; Fat 4.4g, of which saturates 1.1g; Cholesterol 69mg; Calcium 15mg; Fibre 0.2g; Sodium 62mg.

Chocolate Pavlova with Passion Fruit Cream

This winter meringue dish has a delicious chewy centre that is hard to resist.

For the filling
150g/5oz plain (semisweet)
   chocolate, chopped into
   small pieces
250ml/8fl oz/1 cup double
   (heavy) cream
150g/5oz/²⁄₃ cup Greek
   (US strained plain) yogurt
2.5ml/½ tsp vanilla extract
4 passion fruit

Serves 6
4 egg whites
200g/7oz/1 cup caster
   (superfine) sugar
20ml/4 tsp cornflour (cornstarch)
45g/1³⁄₄oz/3 tbsp unsweetened
   cocoa powder
5ml/1 tsp vinegar
chocolate leaves, to decorate

1 Preheat oven to 140°C/275°F/Gas 1. Cut a piece of baking parchment to fit a baking sheet. Draw on a 23cm/9in circle.

2 Whisk the egg whites in a clean, grease-free bowl until stiff. Gradually whisk in the sugar and continue to whisk until the mixture is stiff again. Whisk in the cornflour, cocoa and vinegar.

3 Place the baking parchment upside down on the baking sheet. Spread the mixture over the circle; make a slight dip in the centre. Bake for 1½–2 hours.

4 Make the filling. Melt the chocolate in a heatproof bowl over barely simmering water, then remove from the heat and cool slightly. In a separate bowl, whip the cream with the yogurt and vanilla extract until thick. Fold 60ml/4 tbsp into the chocolate, then set both mixtures aside.

5 Halve all the passion fruit and scoop out the pulp with a spoon. Stir half into the plain cream mixture. Carefully transfer the meringue shell to a serving plate. Fill with the passion fruit cream, then spoon over the chocolate mixture and the remaining passion fruit pulp. Decorate with chocolate leaves. Serve immediately.

Winter Cheesecake with a Pomegranate Glaze

This cake is the ideal recipe for winter pomegranates.

75g/3oz/²⁄₃ cup icing
   (confectioners') sugar, sifted
200ml/7fl oz/scant 1 cup
   coconut cream
2 egg whites

Serves 8
225g/8oz oat biscuits (crackers)
75g/3oz/6 tbsp unsalted
   butter, melted

For the topping
2 pomegranates, peeled and
   seeds separated
grated rind and juice of 1 orange
30ml/2 tbsp caster
   (superfine) sugar
15ml/1 tbsp arrowroot, mixed to a
   paste with 30ml/2 tbsp Kirsch
red food colouring (optional)

For the filling
45ml/3 tbsp orange juice
15ml/1 tbsp powdered gelatine
250g/9oz/generous 1 cup
   mascarpone cheese
200g/7oz/scant 1 cup full-fat
   soft cheese

1 Grease a 23cm/9in springform cake tin (pan). Crumb the biscuits in a food processor or blender. Add the butter and process briefly. Spoon into the tin, press in well, then chill.

2 Make the filling. Pour the orange juice into a heatproof bowl, sprinkle the gelatine on top and set aside for 5 minutes. Place the bowl in a pan of hot water; stir until the gelatine dissolves.

3 Beat together both cheeses and the icing sugar, then beat in the coconut cream. Whisk the egg whites in a grease-free bowl to soft peaks. Stir the melted gelatine into the coconut mixture and fold in the egg whites. Pour over the base and chill until set.

4 Make the topping. Place the pomegranate seeds in a pan and add the orange rind and juice and sugar. Bring to the boil, then lower the heat, cover and simmer for 5 minutes. Add the arrowroot paste and heat, stirring, until thickened. Stir in a few drops of food colouring, if using. Leave to cool.

5 Pour the glaze over the top of the set cheesecake, then chill. Remove from the tin and cut into slices to serve.

Chocolate Pavlova Energy 541kcal/2260kJ; Protein 7.3g; Carbohydrate 56.4g, of which sugars 52.3g; Fat 33.6g, of which saturates 20.4g; Cholesterol 59mg; Calcium 96mg; Fibre 1.9g; Sodium 146mg.
Winter Cheesecake Energy 407kcal/1702kJ; Protein 8.2g; Carbohydrate 37.3g, of which sugars 26.1g; Fat 26.1g, of which saturates 15.2g; Cholesterol 56mg; Calcium 57mg; Fibre 1.1g; Sodium 336mg.

Chocolate Mandarin Trifle

Rich chocolate custard is combined with seasonal mandarin oranges to make a trifle that is utterly delectable and impossible to resist.

Serves 6–8
4 trifle sponges
14 amaretti
60ml/4 tbsp Amaretto di Saronno
 or sweet sherry
8 mandarin oranges

For the custard
200g/7oz plain (semisweet)
 chocolate, broken into squares

25g/1oz/2 tbsp cornflour
 (cornstarch) or custard powder
25g/1oz/2 tbsp caster
 (superfine) sugar
2 egg yolks
200ml/7fl oz/scant 1 cup milk
250g/9oz/generous 1 cup
 mascarpone

For the topping
250g/9oz/generous 1 cup
 mascarpone or fromage frais
chocolate shapes
mandarin slices

1 Break up the trifle sponges and place them in a large glass serving dish. Crumble the amaretti over and then sprinkle with Amaretto or sweet sherry.

2 Squeeze the juice from two of the mandarins and sprinkle into the dish. Segment the rest and put in the dish.

3 Make the custard. Melt the chocolate in a heatproof bowl over hot water. In a separate bowl, mix the cornflour or custard powder, sugar and egg yolks to a smooth paste.

4 Heat the milk in a pan until almost boiling, then pour in a steady stream on to the egg mixture, stirring constantly. Return to the pan and simmer until the custard is thick and smooth.

5 Stir in the mascarpone until melted, then add the melted chocolate; mix well. Spread over the trifle, cool, then chill to set.

6 To finish, spread the mascarpone or fromage frais over the custard, then decorate with chocolate shapes and the remaining mandarin slices just before serving.

Pineapple Custard

These pineapple crème caramels are the perfect winter dinner party dessert. They are very easy to make, especially if you buy prepared fresh pineapple from the supermarket.

Serves 6
350g/12oz peeled fresh
 pineapple, chopped

150g/5oz/²⁄₃ cup caster
 (superfine) sugar
4 eggs, lightly beaten

For the caramel
60ml/4 tbsp granulated
 (white) sugar
juice of 1 lime

1 Put the pineapple in a blender or food processor and process until smooth. Scrape the purée into a pan and add the sugar. Cook for 5 minutes or until reduced by one-third. The mixture should be thick but not jam-like, so add a little water if it is too thick. Transfer to a bowl and leave to cool.

2 Meanwhile make the caramel. Place the granulated sugar in a heavy pan over medium heat. As the sugar caramelizes around the edges, shake the pan to mix the sugar, but do not stir.

3 Remove the pan from the heat as soon as all the sugar has dissolved and the caramel has become golden brown. Immediately stir in the lime juice, taking care not to burn yourself. The hot caramel will spit when the lime juice is added, but this will stop. Divide the caramel among six ramekins and turn them so that they are coated evenly.

4 Preheat the oven to 180°C/350°F/Gas 4. Stir the eggs into the cool pineapple mixture. Divide the mixture equally among the ramekins. Place the moulds in a roasting pan and pour in warm water to come halfway up their sides. Cover with foil and bake for 45 minutes, until set. Allow to cool.

5 Just before serving, unmould the custards directly on to dessert plates. Loosen the edges of the custards with a knife, invert a dessert plate on top of each mould and quickly turn both over. Serve immediately.

Chocolate Trifle Energy 569kcal/2394kJ; Protein 12.5g; Carbohydrate 80.3g, of which sugars 61.3g; Fat 23.1g, of which saturates 12.8g; Cholesterol 135mg; Calcium 162mg; Fibre 2.9g; Sodium 115mg.
Pineapple Custard Energy 211kcal/895kJ; Protein 4.6g; Carbohydrate 42.5g, of which sugars 42.5g; Fat 3.8g, of which saturates 1g; Cholesterol 127mg; Calcium 48mg; Fibre 0.7g; Sodium 50mg.

Vanilla Snow

While a good-quality vanilla essence is perfectly acceptable for flavouring drinks, a far more aromatic taste will be achieved using a vanilla pod. This simple smoothie is deliciously scented, creamy and thick, and well worth the extravagance of using a whole vanilla pod. Its lovely, snowy whiteness is delightfully speckled with tiny black vanilla seeds.

Makes 3 glasses

1 vanilla pod (bean)
25g/1oz/2 tbsp caster
  (superfine) sugar
3 eating apples
300g/11oz/1⅓ cups natural
  (plain) yogurt

1 Using the tip of a sharp knife, split open the vanilla pod lengthways. Put it in a small pan with the sugar and 75ml/5 tbsp water. Heat until the sugar dissolves, then boil for 1 minute. Remove from the heat and leave to steep for 10 minutes.

2 Cut the apples into large chunks and push through the juicer, then pour the juice into a large bowl or jug (pitcher).

3 Lift the vanilla pod out of the pan and scrape the tiny black seeds back into the syrup. Pour into the apple juice.

4 Add the yogurt to the bowl or jug and whisk well by hand or with an electric mixer until the smoothie is thick and frothy. Pour into glasses and serve.

Cook's Tip
Like most smoothies, this one should ideally be served well chilled. Either use apples and yogurt straight from the refrigerator, or you can chill the smoothies briefly before serving. to make a thick, icy version, you could try making the smoothies with frozen yogurt.

Passionata

The combination of ripe passion fruit with sweet caramel is gorgeous in this dreamy milkshake. For convenience, you can easily make the caramel syrup and combine it with the fresh passion fruit juice in advance, so it's all ready for blending with the milk. For the best results, make sure you use really ripe, crinkly passion fruit.

Makes 4 glasses

90g/3½oz/1/2 cup caster
  (superfine) sugar
juice of 2 large oranges
juice of 1 lemon
6 ripe passion fruit, plus
  extra for garnish
550ml/18fl oz/2½ cups
  full cream
(whole) milk
ice cubes

1 Put the sugar in a small, heavy pan with 200ml/7fl oz/scant 1 cup water. Heat gently, stirring with a wooden spoon until the sugar has dissolved.

2 Bring the mixture to the boil and cook, without stirring, for about 5 minutes until the syrup has turned to a deep golden caramel. Watch closely towards the end of the cooking time because caramel can burn very quickly. If this happens, let the caramel cool, then throw it away and start again.

3 When the caramel has turned deep golden, immediately lower the base of the pan into cold water to prevent it from cooking any further.

4 Carefully add the orange and lemon juice, standing back slightly as the mixture will splutter. Return the pan to the heat and cook gently, stirring continuously, to make a smooth syrup. Transfer the syrup to a small heatproof bowl and set aside until it has cooled completely.

5 Cut the passion fruit in half and, using a spoon, scoop out the seeds into a blender or food processor. Add the caramel and milk to the blender and mix until the mixture is smooth and frothy. Pour over ice and serve immediately with a passion fruit garnish.

Vanilla Snow Energy 124kcal/527kJ; Protein 5.4g; Carbohydrate 25.1g, of which sugars 25.1g; Fat 1.1g, of which saturates 0 .5g; Cholesterol 1mg; Calcium 198mg; Fibre 1.6g; Sodium 86mg.
Passionata Energy 197kcal/828kJ; Protein 5.4g; Carbohydrate 33.2g, of which sugars 33.2g; Fat 5.5g, of which saturates 3.5g; Cholesterol 19mg; Calcium 179mg; Fibre 0.8g; Sodium 67mg.

Pomegranate Plus

Pomegranates have an exotic and distinctive flavour that is quite delicious. A reddish skin is usually a sign that the seeds inside will be vibrant and sweet. Pomegranate juice makes a delicious base for this treat of a juice, which is mildly spiced with a hint of ginger.

Serves 2
2 pomegranates
4 fresh figs
15g/½oz fresh root
  ginger, peeled
10ml/2 tsp lime juice
ice cubes and lime wedges,
  to serve

1 Halve the pomegranates. Working over a bowl to catch the juices, pull away the skin to remove the seeds.

2 Quarter the figs and roughly chop the ginger. Push the figs and ginger through a juicer. Push the pomegranate seeds through, reserving a few for decoration. Stir in the lime juice. Pour over ice cubes and lime wedges, then serve.

Ruby Dreamer

Fresh figs are at their best in winter when ruby oranges are also in season.

15ml/1 tbsp dark muscovado
  (molasses) sugar
30–45ml/2–3 tbsp lemon juice
crushed ice

Makes 2 glasses
6 large ripe figs
4 ruby oranges

1 Cut off the hard, woody tips from the stalks of the figs, then use a sharp knife to cut each fruit in half.

2 Squeeze the oranges and pour the juice into a blender or food processor. Add the figs and sugar. Process well until the mixture is smooth and fairly thick.

3 Add the lemon juice and blend. Pour over the ice and serve.

Foaming Citrus Eggnog

For most of us, eggnog is inextricably associated with the festive season. This version, however, pepped up with orange rind and juice for a lighter, fresher taste, has a much wider appeal. Whether you sip it as a late-night soother, serve it as a wintry dessert or enjoy it as a cosy tipple on a wet afternoon, it's sure to bring a warm, rosy glow to your cheeks.

Makes 2 glasses
2 small oranges
150ml/¼ pint/⅔ cup single
  (light) cream
plenty of freshly grated nutmeg
2.5ml/½ tsp ground cinnamon
2.5ml/½ tsp cornflour (cornstarch)
2 eggs, separated
30ml/2 tbsp light muscovado
  (brown) sugar
45ml/3 tbsp brandy
extra nutmeg, for
  sprinkling (optional)

1 Finely grate the rind from the oranges, then squeeze out the juice and pour it into a jug (pitcher).

2 Put the rind in a small heavy pan with the cream, nutmeg, cinnamon and cornflour. Heat gently over a low heat, stirring frequently until bubbling.

3 Whisk the egg yolks with the sugar, using a handheld whisk.

4 Stir the hot citrus cream mixture into the egg yolks, then return to the pan. Pour in the orange juice and brandy and heat very gently, stirring until slightly thickened.

5 Whisk the egg whites in a large, clean bowl until foamy and light.

6 Strain the cream mixture through a sieve into the whisked whites. Stir gently and pour into heatproof punch cups, handled glasses or mugs. Sprinkle over a little extra nutmeg before serving, if you like.

Cook's Tip
Note that this recipe contains almost raw egg.

Pomegranate Plus Energy 224kcal/951kJ; Protein 3.4g; Carbohydrate 52.3g, of which sugars 52.3g; Fat 1.6g, of which saturates 0g; Cholesterol 0mg; Calcium 233mg; Fibre 6.9g; Sodium 58mg.
Ruby Dreamer Energy 417kcal/1776kJ; Protein 7.2g; Carbohydrate 97.8g, of which sugars 97.8g; Fat 2.5g, of which saturates 0g; Cholesterol 0mg; Calcium 443mg; Fibre 13.8g; Sodium 96mg.
Citrus Eggnog Energy 375kcal/1566kJ; Protein 9.1g; Carbohydrate 29.6g, of which sugars 29.6g; Fat 19.9g, of which saturates 10.7g; Cholesterol 232mg; Calcium 112mg; Fibre 0.1g; Sodium 98mg.

Index